LEAN AND GREEN COOKBOOK FOR BEGINNERS 2022

1200-Day Fueling Hacks & Lean and Green Recipes Ready in Less Than 30 Munutes to Help you Keep Healthly and Lose Weight. Includes 5&1 and 4&2&1 Meal Plan

Judy Gambino

Table of Contents

CHICKEN AND POULTRY

1. Medifast Chicken Stir Fry 8
2. Lean Green Chicken Soup 8
3. Teriyaki Chicken Meal Prep 9
4. Lean Green Chicken Pesto Pasta 9
5. All Green Chicken Fritters 10
6. Spicy Green Beans Chicken Skillet 10
7. Vegan Teriyaki Chicken & Broccoli Recipe 11
8. Green Chicken Enchilada Casserole 11
9. Green Chiles Chicken Squash Boats 12
10. Chopped Green Chicken Salad Recipe 13
11. Meal Prep Baked Lime Chicken Bowls 13
12. Green Puree With Chicken 14
13. Green Chicken Chili 14
14. Easy Sweet And Sour Chicken 15
15. One-Pot Chicken & Lentils 15
16. Chicken Fajitas 16
17. Keto Green Bean And Chicken Stir Fry 17
18. Garlic Chicken With Zoodles 17
19. Skinny Chicken Salad 18
20. Healthy Chicken Stir Fry 18
21. Green Chicken + Veggie Soup 19
22. Chicken Fajita Lettuce Wraps 20
23. Chicken And Green Beans 20
24. 20 Minute Meal-Prep Chicken, Rice And Broccoli 21
25. Spinach Salad With Chicken And Farro 22
26. One Skillet Italian Chicken 22
27. Chicken Pad Thai Recipe 23
28. Clean And Green Chicken Salad 24
29. Chicken And Green Bean Stir Fry 24
30. All Green Chicken Fritters 25
31. Buffalo Chicken Pepper Nachos 25
32. Green Chicken Chili 26
33. Healthy Mongolian Chicken 26
34. Green Chicken Enchilada Cauliflower Casserole – Low Carb 27
35. Keto green bean and chicken stir fry 27
36. Chicken Soup With Greens 28
37. Mexican Chicken Soup 29
38. Asian Chicken Cabbage Soup Recipe 29
39. Greek Lemon Chicken Soup (Avgolemono) 30
40. Instant Pot Chicken Curry (Green!) 30
41. Perfect Baked Chicken Thighs 31
42. Thai Chicken Satay With Peanut Sauce 32
43. Thai Cashew Chicken 32
44. Ginger Lime Chicken And Noodles 33
45. Cashew Chicken & Cauliflower Rice 33
46. Mediterranean Roasted Chicken With Lemon Dill Radishes 34
47. Chicken With Garlic And Spring Onion Cream 34
48. Creamy Skillet Chicken And Asparagus 35
49. Toasted Sesame Ginger Chicken 36
50. Pan Seared Balsamic Chicken And Vegetables ... 36
51. Surf And Turk Burgers 37
52. Tex Mex Turkey Stuffed Poblanos 37
53. Lean Green Chicken Soup 38

VEGETARIAN RECIPES

54. 10 Minute Lean & Green Tofu Stir-Fry 39
55. Calabacitas Recipe (Con Queso) 39
56. Heavenly Green Beans And Garlic 40

57. Roasted Garlic Zoodles 40
58. Healthy Baked Zucchini Fritters 41
59. Wild Garlic Soup 41
60. Salsa Verde With Capers 42
61. Forager's Nettle Pesto 42
62. Winter Coleslaw With Barberries 43
63. Lingonberry Sauce 43
64. Ackee Stir-Fry 44
65. Healthy Cream Of Broccoli Soup 44
66. Chipotle Guacamole Deviled Eggs 45
67. The Easiest Vegan Pad Thai 45
68. The Best Vegan Pesto Recipe 46
69. Kale Pesto With Cashew And Parmesan 46
70. Vegan Broccoli Pesto Pasta 47
71. Vegan Zuppa Toscana 48
72. Pumpkin And Kale With Creamy Polenta 48
73. The Best Vegan Corn Chowder 49
74. Cauldron Curry 50
75. Vegan Zucchini Quinoa Sushi Rolls 51
76. Green Shakshuka 51
77. Hummus With Basil Cilantro Oil 52
78. Spring Pesto Green Beans 53
79. Pesto Zucchini Noodles Shrimps & Feta 53
80. Baked Beet Falafel Vegan Quinoa Bowl 54
81. Spring Vegetable Zoodle Pasta 55
82. Vegan Potato Leek Soup 55
83. Green Pizza With Herbed Vegan Cashew Cheese 56
84. Green Goddess Vegan Broccoli Soup 57
85. Lean Green Burger 57
86. Lean Green Lettuce Tacos 58
87. Spicy Steamed Greens With Hemp Seeds 58
88. Summer Zoodle Primavera 59
89. Lean Green Bean Salad 59
90. Green Salad With Beets, Oranges & Avocado 60
91. Avocado Cream Of Mushroom Soup 60
92. Raw Curry Cauliflower Soup 61
93. Chlorophyll-Rich Green Soup 61

SEAFOOD RECIPES

94. Smoky Shrimp Chipotle 62
95. Seared Scallops in Creamy Garlic Sauce 62
96. Tender And Tasty Fish Tacos 63
97. Summer Shrimp Primavera 63
98. Garlic Shrimp & Broccoli 64
99. Spinach Pesto With Couscous And Shrimp 65
100. Pea & Mint Soup With Thai Shrimp Skewers 65
101. Skewered Shrimp With Leeks And Yellow Squash 66
102. Thai Sweet Chili Salmon Soba Noodles 66
103. Easy Healthy Cucumber Tomato Avocado Salad Recipe 67
104. Vegan Scallops With Spring Greens 68
105. Mediterranean Chopped Salad With Shrimp 68
106. Lemony Spinach & Salmon Fusilli 69

SMOOTHIES

107. Lean & Green Smoothie 69
108. 41. Superfood Green Smoothie 70
109. Tasty Lean Green Smoothie 70
110. Slim Down Greens Smoothie 71
111. Green Keto Smoothie 71
112. Non-Dairy Lean Mean Fighting Machine Smoothie Recipe 72
113. 46. Green Apple Smoothie 72

114. Lean, Mean, Green Machine Tropical Smoothie 73
115. Orange And Pineapple Green Smoothie 73
116. Green Protein Detox Smoothie 74
117. Glowing Green Detox Smoothie 74
118. Peaches And Cream Oatmeal Green Smoothie.. 75
119. Berry Delicious Detox Diet Smoothie 75
120. Kale And Apple Green Detox Smoothie............. 76
121. Avocado Detox Smoothie 76
122. Super Green Smoothie Bowl 77
123. Simple Green Acai Smoothie 77
124. Healing Simple Green Smoothie........................ 78
125. The Lean Green Lime Machine 78
126. Weight Loss Green Smoothie 79
127. Lean Green Peach Smoothie 79
128. The Best Green Smoothie................................... 80
129. Low-Carb Green Smoothie 80
130. Lean Green Protein Juice................................... 81
131. Green Smoothie For Beginners 81

SALADS

132. Tabouleh 82
133. Low Carb Potato Salad....................................... 82
134. The Lean Green Kale Bowl................................. 83
135. Cauliflower Tabbouleh.. 84
136. The Ultimate Wedge Salad Recipe 84
137. Spring Green Salad 85
138. Detox Salad... 86
139. Healthy Taco Salad Recipe................................. 86
140. Simple Kale Spinach Salad With Avocado Green Goddess Dressing 87
141. Lean Beef Taco Salad 87
142. Avocado Chicken Salad...................................... 88

143. Ultimate Garden Salad Recipe 89
144. Medifast Lean And Green Recipe 89
145. Healthy Lunch Salad... 90
146. Asian-Style Tuna Salad Recipe 90
147. Salmon Salad.. 91
148. Simple Taco Salad 91
149. Skinny Chicken Salad... 92
150. Lean Green Chicken Pesto Pasta....................... 92
151. Easy Healthy Taco Salad Recipe With Ground Beef 93
152. High-Protein Chicken Salad................................ 93
153. Creamy Cucumber Salad.................................... 94
154. Healthy Turkey Lettuce Wraps 94

SNACKS

155. Zucchini Tart With Ricotta And Herbs................. 95
156. Avocado Goat Cheese Cucumber Appetizers 95
157. Muffins florentine recipe 96
158. Spinach Crepes With Pan-Roasted Vegetables... 96
159. Kale Kefir Pancakes 97
160. Okonomiyaki 98
161. Holy Guacamole Recipe 99
162. Crispy Kohlrabi Slaw... 99
163. Lemon Dill Roasted Radishes 100
164. Low Carb Sloppy Joes....................................... 100
165. Fresh Lime Crema 101
166. Fresh Pico De Gallo 101
167. Tex-Mex Seared Salmon 102

FUELING HACKS RECIPES

168. Spring Green Smoothie Breakfast Drink 102
169. Nectarine And Avocado Smoothie.................... 103

170. Morning Green Juice 103
171. Peanut Butter Green Smoothie 104
172. Pistachio Muffins 104
173. Skillet Mexican Zucchini 105
174. Coconut Green Smoothie 105
175. Tiramisu Shake 106
176. Cumin and Cheese Hack 106
177. Cauliflower Wings 107
178. Neapolitan Popsicles 107
179. Mint Chocolate Muffins 108
180. Zucchini Bread 108
181. Oatmeal Cookies 109
182. Mint Cookies 109
183. Shrimp Salad 110
184. Peanut Butter Cookies 110
185. Pumpkin Pie Frappe 111
186. Peanut Butter Brownie 111
187. Pancake Cinnamon Buns 112
188. Cinnamon Roll 112
189. Pumpkin Pie Custard 113
190. Chocolate Cookies 113
191. Brownie Ice Cream 114
192. Chocolate Coffee Muffins 114
193. Pancake Muffins 115
194. Pecan Ice Cream 115
195. Chocolate Peanut Cup 116
196. Peanut Brownie and Greek Yogurt 116
197. Cheese Tomato Sandwich 117
198. Honey Cinnamon Oatmeal 117
199. Peanut Butter Cups 118
200. Tomato Bread 118

LEAN AND GREEN MEAL PLAN 5&1

LEAN AND GREEN MEAL PLAN 4&2&1

What is Lean and Green Diet?

Lean & Green is a weight loss or maintenance plan that prescribes eating a mix of purchased, processed food called "fuelings" and homemade "lean and green" meals. There's no counting carbs or calories. Instead, followers add water to powdered food or unwrap a bar as part of six-or-so mini-meals per day. Lean & Green also offers guidance from coaches to help you learn their trademarked "Habits of Health." The plan additionally recommends doing about 30 minutes of moderate-intensity exercise per day.

" Lean & Green works because it's simple and easy to follow. Five of your daily meals are Lean & Green Fuelings. You'll choose from more than 60 delicious, convenient, nutritionally interchangeable, scientifically-designed Fuelings. Your body will enter a gentle, but efficient fat-burning state, essential for losing weight. Each Fueling contains high-quality protein which helps retain lean muscle mass, and probiotic cultures, which help support digestive health, as part of a balanced diet and healthy lifestyle."

How Does The "Lean & Green" Diet Work?

The "Lean and Green" diet subscribes to the idea that eating several small meals or snacks every day leads to manageable and sustained weight loss, and ultimately habit change. The thinking is that instead of eating three huge meals every day, you'll never get that hungry because you're eating six or seven small, filling, and nutritious meals throughout the day. While this may work well for some people, we're all different and there isn't a ton of convincing research to back this method up. The efficacy of eating small meals and found that, ultimately, weight loss is directly related to restricting calories, and the timing and sizing of the meals themselves don't have a meaningful impact on weight loss.

When it comes to successful long-term weight loss, experts seem to agree on one thing: The emotional and behavioral aspects of eating not just the specific meals you're eating are incredibly important. They also stress the importance of looking at whole-body wellness as a path to safe and sustainable weight loss.

What To Eat

- Lean & Green fuelings
- Lean meats
- Greens and other non-starchy vegetables
- Healthy fats
- Low-fat dairy, fresh fruit, and whole grains (on some plans)

What Not To Eat

- Indulgent desserts
- High-calorie additions
- Sugary beverages
- Alcohol

What Kinds Of Foods Can I Eat On The Lean & Green Diet?

- Lean meats, like turkey, lamb, or chicken
- Fish and shellfish, like salmon, crab, shrimp
- Tofu
- Low-carb veggies, including spinach, cauliflower, mushrooms, and cabbage
- Healthy fats, like avocados and pistachios
- Sugar-free beverages and snacks, including coffee and tea
- Vegetable oils
- Eggs

What Foods Should I Avoid On The "Lean and Green" Diet?

- Fried foods
- Refined grains, like white bread, pasta, and white rice
- Alcohol
- Butter
- Coconut oil
- Milk
- Cheese
- Soda, fruit juice, and other sugar-sweetened beverages

Pros And Cons

Pros
- Packaged products offer convenience
- Achieves rapid weight loss
- Takes guesswork out of what to eat
- Offers social support

Cons
- High monthly cost
- Includes a lot of processed food
- Weight loss may be unsustainable

- Calorie restriction may leave you hungry or fatigued
- Mealtimes can become boring or feel isolating

Health Benefits

Lean & Green's program might be a good fit for you if you want a diet plan that is clear and easy to follow, that will help you lose weight quickly, and offers built-in social support.

- **Packaged Products Offer Convenience**

Lean & Green's shakes, soups, and all other meal replacement products are delivered directly to your door, a level of convenience that many other diets do not offer. Although you will need to shop for your ingredients for "lean and green" meals, the home delivery option for "Lean and Green"'s "fuelings" saves time and energy. Once the products arrive, they're easy to prepare and make excellent grab-and-go meals.

- **Achieves Rapid Weight Loss**

Most healthy people require around 1600 to 3000 calories per day to maintain their weight. Restricting that number to as low as 800 essentially guarantees weight loss for most people. Lean & Green's 5 & 1 plan is designed for quick weight loss, making it a solid option for someone with a medical reason to shed pounds fast.

- **Eliminates Guesswork**

Some people find that the hardest part of dieting is the mental effort required to figure out what to eat each day—or even at each meal. "Lean and Green" alleviates the stress of meal planning and "decision fatigue" by offering users clear-cut approved foods with "fuelings" and guidelines for "lean and green" meals.

- **Health Risks**

There are also some potential downsides to "Lean and Green"'s plan, especially if you are worried about cost, flexibility, and variety.

- **Includes Processed Food**

Although "Lean and Green"'s "fuelings" are engineered with interchangeable nutrients, they're still undeniably processed foods, which may be a turn off for some users. Nutrition research has shown eating a lot of processed food can have detrimental effects on one's health, so this aspect of the diet plan may pose a disadvantage.

- **Weight Loss May Not Be Sustainable**

One challenge familiar to anyone on a diet is determining how to maintain weight loss once they've completed the program. The same goes for Lean & Green's program. When users go back to eating regular meals instead of the plan's meal replacements, they might find that the weight they lost is quickly regained.

- **Effects Of Calorie Restriction**

Even though Lean & Green's diet plan emphasizes eating frequently throughout the day, each of its "fuelings" only provides 110 calories. "Lean and green" meals are also low in calories. When you're eating fewer calories in general, you may find the plan leaves you hungry and unsatisfied. You may also feel more easily fatigued and even irritable.

- **Boredom And Isolation At Mealtimes**

Lean & Green's reliance on meal replacements can interfere with the social aspects of preparing and eating food. Users might find it awkward or disappointing to have a shake or bar at family mealtime or when dining out with friends.

Lean & Green Fuelings

The majority of the food you'll eat on the "Lean and Green" Diet will take the form of its pre-packaged "feelings." According to "Lean and Green"'s online guide, you can choose from over 60 soups, bars, shakes, pretzels, and other products (even brownies!) as meal replacements.

The company states that "each item has a nearly identical nutrition profile," which means they can be eaten interchangeably.

The "lean and green" meals you'll prepare need to include a five-to-seven-ounce portion of cooked lean protein. "Lean and Green" distinguishes between lean, leaner, and leanest protein sources using the following examples:

- Lean: Salmon, lamb, or pork chops
- Leaner: Swordfish or chicken breast
- Leanest: Cod, shrimp, and egg whites

"Lean and Green"'s 5 & 1 program allows for two non-starchy vegetables alongside the protein in your "lean and green" meal. The veggies are divided into lower, moderate, and higher carbohydrate categories, with the following as examples:
- Lower carb: Salad greens
- Moderate carb: Cauliflower or summer squash
- Higher Carb: Broccoli or peppers

On the "Lean and Green" 5&1 Plan, the only foods allowed are the "Lean and Green" Fuelings and one Lean and Green Meal per day. These meals consist mostly of lean proteins, healthy fats, and low carb vegetables with a recommended two servings of fatty fish per week. Some low carb condiments and beverages are also allowed in small amounts.

Foods allowed in your daily Lean & Green meal include:

- **Meat:** chicken, turkey, lean beef, game meats, lamb, pork chop or tenderloin, ground meat (at least 85% lean)
- **Fish and shellfish:** halibut, trout, salmon, tuna, lobster, crab, shrimp, scallops
- **Eggs:** whole eggs, egg whites, Egg Beaters
- **Soy products:** only tofu
- **Vegetable oils:** canola, flaxseed, walnut, and olive oil
- **Additional healthy fats:** low carb salad dressings, olives, reduced fat margarine, almonds, walnuts, pistachios, avocado
- **Low carb vegetables:** collard greens, spinach, celery, cucumbers, mushrooms, cabbage, cauliflower, eggplant, zucchini, broccoli, peppers, spaghetti squash, jicama
- **Sugar-free snacks:** popsicles, gelatin, gum, mints
- **Sugar-free beverages:** water, unsweetened almond milk, tea, coffee
- **Condiments and seasonings:** dried herbs, spices, salt, lemon juice, lime juice, yellow mustard, soy sauce, salsa, sugar-free syrup, zero-calorie sweeteners, 1/2 teaspoon only of ketchup, cocktail sauce, or barbecue sauce

A Lean & Green meal includes 5 to 7 ounces of cooked lean protein plus three (3) servings of non-starchy vegetables and up to two (2) servings of healthy fats, depending on your lean protein choices. Enjoy your Lean & Green meal any time of day — whatever works best for your schedule.

How to follow the Lean & Green diet

Initial steps
For weight loss, most people start with the Optimal Weight 5&1 Plan, which is an 800–1,000 calorie regimen said to help you drop 12 pounds (5.4 kg) over 12 weeks.
On this plan, you eat 5 "Lean and Green" Fuelings and 1 Lean and Green meal daily. You're meant to eat 1 meal every 2–3 hours and incorporate 30 minutes of moderate exercise most days of the week.
In total, the Fuelings and meal provide no more than 100 grams of carbs per day.

Lean and Green meals are designed to be high in protein and low in carbs. One meal offers 5–7 ounces (145–200 grams) of cooked lean protein, 3 servings of non-starchy vegetables, and up to 2 servings of healthy fats.
This plan also includes 1 optional snack per day, which must be approved by your coach. Plan-approved snacks include 3 celery sticks, 1/2 cup (60 grams) of sugar-free gelatin, or 1/2 ounce (14 grams) of nuts.

Maintenance phase
Once you reach your desired weight, you enter a 6-week transition phase, which involves slowly increasing calories to no more than 1,550 calories per day and adding in a wider variety of foods, including whole grains, fruits, and low fat dairy.
After 6 weeks, you're meant to move onto the Optimal Health 3&3 Plan, which includes 3 Lean and Green meals and 3 Fuelings daily, plus continued "Lean and Green" coaching.
Those who experience sustained success on the program have the option to become trained as an "Lean and Green" coach

CHICKEN AND POULTRY

1. Medifast Chicken Stir Fry

Minutes To Prepare: 10 Mins
Minutes To Cook: 10 Mins
Ingredients
- 12 oz skinless, boneless chicken breast
- 1 cup chopped red bell pepper
- 1 cup chopped green bell pepper
- 8 oz (1 cup) broccoli slaw
- 1/2 cup chicken broth
- 2 tbs low sodium no-carb soy sauce
- 1 tsp crushed red pepper

Instructions
1. Sautee peppers and broccoli slaw in chicken broth.
2. Add soy sauce, add chicken, and red pepper.
3. Cook for a few more minutes until peppers are tender.

Nutritional info
Total Fat: 1.2 G Cholesterol: 27.5 Mg Sodium: 873.4 Mg Total Carbs: 15.4 G Dietary Fiber: 7.0 G Protein: 15.1 G

2. Lean Green Chicken Soup

Prep Time: 15 Minutes
Cook Time: 25 Minutes
Total Time: 40 Minutes
Ingredients
- 2 quarts chicken broth or stock
- 1 1/2 pounds boneless, skinless chicken breast
- 2 celery stalks, chopped
- 2 cups green beans, cut into 1-inch pieces
- 1 1/2 cups peas, fresh or frozen
- 2 cups asparagus, cut into 1-inch pieces, tops, and middles
- 1 cup diced green onions
- 4-6 cloves garlic, minced
- 2 cups fresh spinach leaves, chopped and packed
- 1 bunch watercress, chopped with large stems removed
- 1/2 cup fresh parsley leaves, chopped
- 1/3 cup fresh basil leaves, chopped
- 1 teaspoon salt
- 1/2 teaspoon ground black pepper

Instructions
1. Pour the chicken broth into a large pot, and set over medium-high heat. Add the chicken breasts and bring them to a simmer. Cook for 15 minutes.
2. Add the celery, green beans, peas, asparagus, onions, garlic, salt, and pepper. Simmer for 5-10 minutes until tender, then remove from heat.
3. Remove the chicken breasts and shred with two forks or chop into bite-sized pieces. Return to the pot.
4. Stir in the spinach, watercress, parsley, and basil. Taste, then salt and pepper as needed.

Nutritional Value
Carbohydrates: 7g, Protein: 15g, Fat: 2g, Saturated Fat: 0g, Cholesterol: 36mg, Sodium: 852mg, Potassium:

556mg, Fiber: 2g, Sugar: 2g, Vitamin A: 1345iu, Vitamin C: 30.3mg, Calcium: 52mg, Iron: 1.9mg

3. Teriyaki Chicken Meal Prep

Prep Time: 10 Minutes
Cook Time: 25 Minutes

Ingredients
- 1 cup brown rice uncooked
- 1 lb boneless chicken breasts cut into 1" pieces
- 3 cups snap peas
- 3 tbsp soy sauce i used bragg liquid aminos
- 3 tbsp maple syrup or honey
- 6 tbsp water
- 1 tsp rice or white vinegar
- 1 tbsp cornstarch
- 2 large garlic cloves grated & divided
- 2 tsp ginger minced & divided
- 1 green onion sprig finely chopped
- 2 tsp sesame seeds
- 2 tsp avocado oil divided

Instructions
1. Cook brown rice as per package instructions.
2. In the meanwhile, cut chicken using scissors right in the packaging tray.
3. Preheat a large ceramic non-stick skillet on medium-high heat and swirl oil to coat. Add chicken and cook for 7 minutes, stirring occasionally.
4. In a small bowl, add soy sauce, maple syrup, water, vinegar, and cornstarch; whisk well (cornstarch settles to the bottom quickly, so make sure to whisk well again before adding to the skillet). To the skillet, add 1 garlic clove, 1 tsp ginger, half of the sauce, and cook until sauce has thickened and is sticking to chicken (about 3 minutes). Divide between 4 glass meal prep containers
5. Return skillet to medium heat and add remaining 1 tsp of oil, snap peas, 1 garlic clove, and 1 tsp of ginger; cook for 1 minute, stirring occasionally.
6. Add remaining sauce (whisk again). Cook until the sauce has thickened, about 1 minute. Divide between 4 meal prep containers. Then add rice to each container.
7. Sprinkle chicken and snap peas with sesame seeds and green onion.

Nutrition Value
Carbohydrates: 58g Protein: 30g Fat: 15g Saturated Fat: 4g Cholesterol: 73mg Sodium: 479mg Potassium: 545mg Fiber: 4g Sugar: 16g Vitamin A: 893iu Vitamin C: 45mg Calcium: 72mg Iron: 4mg

4. Lean Green Chicken Pesto Pasta

Prep Time: 15 Minutes
Total Time: 30 Minutes

Ingredients
- Kale pesto
- 3 cups (48g) raw kale (stems removed)
- 2 cup (12g) fresh basil
- 2 tablespoons (28g) olive oil
- 3 tablespoons lemon juice
- 3 garlic cloves
- ¼ teaspoon salt
- Pasta salad
- 2 cups (280g) cooked chicken breast (diced)
- 6 oz (176g) uncooked "barilla" rotini chickpea pasta
- 1 cup (20g) arugula or baby spinach
- 3oz (84g) "bel gioioso" fresh mozzarella (diced)

Instructions
1. Make the pesto by adding the kale, basil, olive oil, garlic cloves, lemon juice, and salt to a food processor. Blend until smooth. Season to taste with additional salt and pepper.

2. Cook pasta according to package directions. Strain, reserving ¼ cup cooking liquid.
3. In a large bowl, mix the cooked pasta, diced chicken, pesto, arugula or spinach, reserved pasta liquid, and mozzarella and toss until combined. Sprinkle with extra chopped basil or red pepper flakes (if desired).
4. Serve chilled or warm. This pasta salad is delicious on its own, as a salad mix-in, or as a side! Store leftovers in an airtight container in the refrigerator for 3-5 days. Enjoy!

Nutrition facts
Carbs: 22.5g Protein: 20.5g Fat: 10g

5.	All Green Chicken Fritters

Time To Make: 30 Mins
Ingredients
- Fritters
- 1 cup grated courgette
- 1 quantity basic fritter mix
- 7oz lean cooked chicken, diced
- 1 head broccoli, cut in florets, steamed and chopped
- 4 spears asparagus or 4oz green beans, steamed and chopped
- 2 cloves garlic, crushed
- 1 teaspoon dried mixed herbs
- 4 tablespoons fresh coriander or basil
- Spray oil
- 2 cups cherry tomatoes
- 6 radishes, trimmed
- Spray oil
- 2 cups rocket
- ⅓ cup low-fat yogurt
- 4 fresh coriander or basil leaves, chopped

Instructions
1. Combine half the courgettes and the rest of the fritter ingredients.
2. Heat oven to 360°f. Place tomatoes and radishes on a baking tray, spray with oil and bake for 15 minutes.
3. Spray a non-stick pan with spray oil and place over medium heat. Cook 2-3 fritters at a time, for 2-3 minutes on each side or until golden brown.
4. Mix yogurt and herbs together. Serve the fritters with roasted vegetables, remaining courgette, rocket, and yogurt on the side. Garnish with coriander or basil.

Nutrition Info
Protein: 34g Total Fat: 11g Saturated Fat: 2g
Carbohydrates: 45g Sugars: 10g Dietary Fiber: 10g
Sodium: 390mg Calcium: 300mg Iron: 4mg

6.	Spicy Green Beans Chicken Skillet

Total Time: 25 Minutes
Ingredients
- 1 lb. Free-range organic boneless chicken breasts
- Salt and ground fresh black pepper
- 1 teaspoon paprika
- 1 teaspoon onion powder
- 1 tablespoon lemon juice
- 1 +1 tablespoon olive oil
- 3 garlic cloves - minced
- ½ teaspoon red hot chili pepper - chopped (for less heat remove the seed of the red hot chili pepper)
- 2-3 cups green beans - trimmed and cut into small pieces
- 2 tablespoons chicken broth or water - if necessary

Instructions
1. On a plastic board, cut the chicken into small pieces and season with salt and pepper, paprika, onion powder, and lemon juice.
2. Mix everything well.
3. In a skillet over medium heat, add 1 tablespoon of olive oil and after 2 minutes add the chicken.
4. Sauté the chicken for about 7-10 minutes or until it is cooked through. Don't forget to stir well. Set chicken aside.
5. In the same skillet, add another 1-tablespoon of olive oil, garlic, and red hot chili pepper. Sauté for 30 seconds and be careful to not burn the garlic.
6. Add green beans and sauté for 3 minutes. Stir occasionally.
7. Add chicken broth and close the skillet and cook for about 3-5 minutes or so. The time will depend on how crispy you prefer your green beans to be.
8. Bring the chicken back to the skillet, give a nice stir and serve immediately.

Nutritional value
Carbohydrates: 10g Protein: 26g Fat: 13g Saturated Fat: 2g Polyunsaturated Fat: 1g Monounsaturated Fat: 7g Cholesterol: 59mg Sodium: 390mg Potassium: 488mg Fiber: 3g Sugar: 4g Calcium: 43mg Iron: 8mg

7. Vegan Teriyaki Chicken & Broccoli Recipe

Prep Time: 5 Mins
Cook Time: 13 Mins
Total Time: 18 Mins

Ingredients
- 1 10 oz pkg plant-based chicken strips
- 2 tbsp teriyaki sauce
- 1 tbsp fresh garlic minced
- 1/2 cup yellow onion diced
- 2 cups broccoli
- 1/4 cup fresh scallions sliced
- 2 tbsp water

Instructions
1. Chop the broccoli into bite-sized pieces after rinsing it well.
2. In a medium-sized skillet, cook the garlic and onion in the water, over medium-high heat, for five minutes. Stir the mixture frequently.
3. Add the chicken strips, teriyaki sauce, and broccoli, and continue cooking for eight more minutes.
4. Serve hot topped with freshly sliced scallions.

8. Green Chicken Enchilada Casserole

Prep Time: 5 Mins
Cook Time: 25 Mins
Total Time: 30 Mins

Ingredients
- 6 whole-wheat tortillas (large burrito / wrap size)
- 1 15-oz can white beans
- 1 12-oz bag shredded cheese – mexican blend
- 1 cup shredded monterey jack cheese
- 1 24-oz jar salsa verde
- 2 4-oz cans of green hatch chiles (mild + diced)
- Shredded crockpot salsa chicken
- 1 tbs dried oregano

Toppings
- Whole milk greek yogurt/ sour cream
- Guacamole (love the single-serving containers for meal prep!)

- Cholula hot sauce
- Fresh cilantro

Instructions
1. Preheat oven: to 375 degrees
2. Prep casserole ingredients: cut each tortilla in half, set it aside. Open, drain, and rinse beans. Put into a small bowl and stir together with the 2 cans of hatch chiles. Set aside.
3. Layer casserole: for the first layer, place four tortilla halves into the bottom of a 9" x 13" casserole or baking dish, lining up one flat edge (the cut part) against each side of the dish
4. The rounded parts will overlap to cover the center. Add enough salsa verde to coat the tortillas (about a third of the large salsa jar). Use the back of a spoon to spread it around evenly. Then add half of the white bean + green chile mixture, followed by half of the chicken (about 2 chicken breasts worth).
5. Make sure the ingredients are spread out evenly by just pushing them with your hands. Now sprinkle one-third of the bag of cheese over top. · repeat this layer once more for the second layer. · then for the third layer – top with the remaining tortilla halves, and use only half of the remaining salsa in the jar to spread around the top of the tortillas.
6. If you like crispier edges on your enchiladas, then leave an inch around the edge of the pan where you don't put salsa on the tortillas. · now add the remaining mexican cheese blend + the extra cup of monterey jack cheese (which isn't necessary but if you're all about having the gooiest topping situation possible, is highly recommended).
7. Finish by sprinkling with dried oregano.
8. Bake: bake for 23 minutes at 375. Then if you like a golden bubbly topping, crank your oven up to broil (high setting) for 2-3 minutes. Be sure to watch it during those last few minutes as oven temperatures can vary greatly + you don't want it to burn!
9. Take out and let cool for 10 minutes before serving. · can store in the fridge in the casserole dish covered with foil for up to a week.

Nutritional Facts
Total Fat: 5.6g Sat Fat: 1.8g Cholesterol: 103mg
Sodium: 155mg Carbohydrates: 0.7g Fiber: 0.2g
Sugar: 0g Protein: 37.2g Calcium: 18mg Iron: 2mg
Potassium: 600mg

9. Green Chiles Chicken Squash Boats

Prep Time: 7 Minutes
Cook Time: 13 Minutes
Total Time: 20 Minutes

Ingredients
- 1 lb lean ground chicken
- 4oz hatch green chiles (mild, canned)
- 1 cup brown & wild rice mix
- 1 tbsp garlic paste
- 10 cherry tomatoes (sliced in half)
- 1/2 tbsp cumin
- 3 tbsp reduced-fat mozzarella (optional)
- Fresh cilantro (chopped)

Instructions
1. Set oven to 405F.
2. Slice yellow squash in half and carve out part of the insides with the seeds.
3. Set a nonstick skillet on medium-high heat. Add garlic paste and ground chicken, then cumin seasoning and cook until chicken is 70% finished. Chop the chicken with a wooden spatula so that it does not bind together.
4. Toss in green chiles and cooked rice. Mix and cook until the chicken is 90% finished.
5. Place the squash halves on a baking sheet.
6. Fill the squash with the chicken and chile mixture.
7. Slice cherry tomatoes in half and place them on top of the meat mixture.
8. Top with mozzarella cheese, about 1/2 tbsp for each boat half.
9. Bake for 20 minutes for cooked yet firm squash.

Nutritional Value
Protein: 19g Fat: 4g Carbs: 15g Fiber: 3g

10. Chopped Green Chicken Salad Recipe

Prep Time: 5 Mins
Cook Time: 15 Mins
Total Time: 20 Mins

Ingredients
- 150 g chicken breast
- 1/4 avocado cubed
- 1/2 bunch broccolini diced into 1cm pieces
- 1 cup baby spinach
- 1/2 cucumber diced
- 1/4 cup coriander fresh roughly chopped
- 1/4 lime juiced
- 1.5 teaspoon extra-virgin olive oil
- 1/2 tablespoon pumpkin seeds

Instructions
For The Chicken
1. Place the chicken in a saucepan and pour over enough water to just cover.
2. Season with sea salt and freshly ground black pepper, then cover with a lid.
3. Bring to the boil over high heat, then reduce the heat to medium and simmer for 5 minutes.
4. Add the broccolini to the pan and continue to simmer for 5 minutes.
5. Remove the lid and the broccolini and stand the chicken in the liquid for a further 5 minutes.
6. Drain and shred the chicken.

For The Salad
7. Arrange the chicken, avocado, broccolini, spinach, cucumber, and coriander around a wide bowl.
8. Add lime juice and olive oil to a small jar and shake to combine.
9. Drizzle the dressing over the salad bowl and sprinkled with pepitas and season with salt and pepper.

Nutrition Facts
Fat: 23g Saturated Fat: 3g Cholesterol: 96mg Sodium: 355mg Potassium: 3852mg Carbohydrates: 48g Fiber: 13g Sugar: 9g Protein 52g

11. Meal Prep Baked Lime Chicken Bowls

Cook Time: 20 Minutes
Total Time: 20 Minutes

Ingredients
- 2-3 lbs. Boneless skinless chicken breasts, cut into cubes
- 6 tbsp. Olive oil
- 3 tbsp. Red wine vinegar
- Juice from 2 limes
- 2 tsp. Chili powder
- 1 tsp. Paprika
- 1 tsp. Garlic powder
- 1 tsp. Kosher salt
- Fresh cracked pepper to taste

Instructions
1. In a large resealable bag, combine olive oil, vinegar, lime juice, chili powder, paprika, garlic powder, salt, and pepper.
2. Cut chicken into cubes and add to the marinade. Toss to coat. Marinate for 2 hours or up to overnight.
3. Preheat oven to 400°f. Pour marinated chicken onto a baking sheet and bake in preheated oven for 20 minutes, or until chicken is cooked through.
4. Serve with cooked quinoa and lemon green beans amandine or roasted brussels sprouts (or other green vegetables). Enjoy!

Nutritional Value
Carbohydrates: 10g Protein: 9g Fat: 18g Saturated Fat: 11g Cholesterol: 52mg Sodium: 289mg Potassium: 511mg Fiber: 2g Sugar: 1g Calcium: 256mg Iron: 2.3mg

12.	Green Puree With Chicken

Prep Time: 5 Minutes
Cook Time: 25 Minutes
Ingredients
- 2 small zucchini, roughly chopped
- 2 apples, peeled, cored, and roughly chopped
- 1-2 cups baby spinach, packed
- 1/2 organic skinless boneless chicken breast
- 1/4 tsp pepper (optional)

Instructions
1. Bring 2 inches of water to a boil in a medium saucepan. Place the chicken in a steamer basket over boiling water, cover, and cook for 10 minutes.
2. Flip the chicken over, sprinkle the pepper onto the chicken, if using. Add the zucchini, apple, and then the spinach on top of the chicken. Cover and cook for 10 additional minutes. Do not mix and keep spinach on top. Let slightly cool. Reserve steamer water.
3. Remove chicken to check for doneness and then roughly chop.
4. Transfer all ingredients into a blender or food processor. For stage 2 puree – blend for 1-2 minutes or until you achieve desired consistency, adding reserved water in 1/4 cup increments if needed. For stage 3 puree – pulse in 5-second intervals until you have achieved the desired chunky consistency, adding reserved water in 1/4 cup increments if needed.

Nutrition Value
Carbohydrates: 1g Protein: 24g Fat: 5g Saturatedfat: 1g Cholesterol: 73mg Sodium: 277mg Potassium: 430mg Fiber: 1g Sugar: 1g Vitamin C: 1mg Calcium: 8mg Iron: 1mg

13.	Green Chicken Chili

Total Time: 10 Minutes
Ingredients
- 1 lg white onion - diced
- 1 yellow bell pepper - diced
- 2 cloves garlic
- 1.5 lbs boneless skinless chicken thighs - cut into 1" pieces
- 1 16 oz jar salsa verde
- 1 15 oz can cannellini beans - rinsed and drained
- 1 32 oz box chicken stock
- Cheese, cilantro, jalapenos, onion, etc. For garnish.

Instructions
1. In a large pot or dutch oven over medium-high heat cook the onion, bell pepper, and garlic in xvi till softened and fragrant - about 3-5 minutes.
2. Add chicken, season with snp, and cook till chicken browns a bit - another 3-5 minutes.
3. Add remaining ingredients, bring to a boil and skim.
4. Cover pot, reduce heat to low, and simmer for about an hour.
5. Garnish with cheese, jalapenos, onions, and sour cream... Enjoy.

Nutrition Facts
Protein: 1.5g Carbohydrates: 10.9g Dietary Fiber: 2.2g Fat: 2.6g Saturated Fat: 0.4g Cholesterol: 3.1mg

Vitamin : C 29.5mg Folate: 56.1mcg Calcium: 22.9mg Iron 0.5mg.

| 14. | Easy Sweet And Sour Chicken |

Prep Time: 15 Minutes
Cook Time: 15 Minutes
Total Time: 30 Minutes

Ingredients
- 1 tbsp groundnut oil divided
- 1 1/2 pounds boneless skinless chicken breasts
- 2 red bell peppers cut into 1-inch chunks
- 1 yellow bell pepper cut into 1-inch chunks
- 1 small yellow onion cut into 1-inch chunks
- 3 garlic cloves minced
- Inch knob of ginger grated or minced
- 1/4 cup low sodium soy sauce or coconut aminos liquid
- 2 tbsp honey
- 2 tbsp worcestershire sauce
- 1 tbsp white vinegar
- 1 tbsp tomato paste
- 2 tbsp cornstarch
- 1 small pineapple or 1/4 from a big pineapple
- 2 tbsp thinly sliced green onion for serving
- 2 tsp toasted sesame seeds for serving
- Optional: cooked rice

Instructions
1. Heat half a tablespoon of oil in a large pan over medium heat.
2. Add prepared veggies and stir fry for 3-4 minutes, until just beginning to get tender. Set aside.
3. To the same preheated skillet add garlic, ginger, and fry for 1 minute.
4. Add in the chicken and cook, stirring frequently, until golden and cooked through.
5. Meanwhile, in a small bowl, combine the soy sauce, honey, worcestershire, vinegar, tomato paste, and cornstarch.
6. Whisk well until cornstarch is fully dissolved.
7. Pour this mixture over the cooked chicken and stir to coat, allowing it to simmer for a couple of minutes; you'll see it begins to thicken almost immediately.
8. Return the cooked veggies to the pan, together with the pineapple chunks.
9. Toss everything to combine and coat with the sauce.
10. Sprinkle with sesame seeds and green onion and serve over cooked rice, if desired.

Nutrition Value
Calories: 294kcal Carbohydrates: 36g Protein: 26g Fat: 6g Saturated Fat: 1g Trans Fat: 1g Cholesterol: 73mg Sodium: 567mg Potassium: 828mg Fiber: 4g Sugar: 24g Calcium: 45mg Iron: 2mg

| 15. | One-Pot Chicken & Lentils |

Prep Time: 5 Min
Cook Time: 25 Min
Duration: 30 Min

Ingredients
- 2 6-oz boneless, skinless chicken breasts, sliced into 1-oz pieces
- 2 tsp curry powder (try: simply organic curry powder)
- 1 1/2 cups dry green lentils, rinsed
- 1 cup nonfat plain greek yogurt
- 1/2 cup chopped fresh cilantro

Pantry Staples:
- Pinch each sea salt and fresh ground black pepper

- 2 tsp olive oil
- 2 cloves garlic, minced
- 1 cup low-sodium chicken broth

Instructions

1. Season chicken with salt and pepper. In a large saucepan or dutch oven, heat oil on medium-high.
2. Add chicken and cook, turning occasionally, for 3 to 4 minutes or until lightly browned.
3. Add curry powder and garlic and cook, stirring, until fragrant, about 1 minute.
4. Add lentils to the saucepan and stir to coat. Stir in broth and 3 cups cold water; bring to a boil.
5. Reduce heat to medium and cook, stirring occasionally, until lentils are tender and most liquid is absorbed, about 30 minutes.
6. Divide evenly among serving bowls, season to taste with salt and pepper, and garnish each with yogurt and 2 tbsp cilantro.

Nutrition Information

Carbohydrate: 45g Cholesterol: 49mg Fat: 5g Fiber: 11g Protein: 42g Saturated Fat: 1g Sodium: 139mg Sugar: 4g

16.	**Chicken Fajitas**

Prep Time: 5 Mins
Cook Time: 25 Mins
Total Time: 30 Mins

Ingredients

- 16 oz boneless skinless chicken breasts
- 1 red bell pepper, cut into strips
- 1 green or poblano pepper, cut into strips
- 1 medium onion, cut into strips
- 3 tbsp lime juice
- 1 tsp ground cumin
- 1 tsp garlic powder
- Pinch ancho or mexican chili powder, to taste
- Salt and pepper to taste
- 2 tsp olive oil
- 8 reduced-carb whole wheat flour tortillas, or corn tortillas

For Garnish:

- 1/2 cup reduced-fat shredded mexican cheese
- Reduced-fat sour cream, optional
- Guacamole, optional

Instructions

1. Marinate the chicken with lime juice, and season with chile powder, salt, pepper, garlic powder, and cumin.
2. Season vegetables with salt and pepper and toss with olive oil.
3. To grill the onions and peppers outside on the grill, use a cast-iron skillet and grill covered over medium heat until tender, about 15 minutes. Or, to cook them indoors, you can use a large skillet on the stove over medium heat for 16 to 18 minutes, covered until the onions and peppers are soft.
4. Heat an outdoor grill or indoor grill pan over medium heat; grill chicken until cooked through, about 8 minutes on each side.
5. Transfer to a cutting board when done and cut into strips. Once cooked, combine with the peppers and onions.
6. Serve immediately with warmed tortillas, cheese, and toppings.

Nutritional Value

Carbohydrates: 27g Protein: 39g Fat: 10.5g Cholesterol: 7.5mg Sodium: 423mg Fiber: 15.5g

17. Keto Green Bean And Chicken Stir Fry

Prep Time: 5 Minutes
Cook Time: 15 Minutes
Total Time: 20 Minutes

Ingredients
- 1 pound boneless, skinless chicken breast, sliced thin
- ½ cup chicken broth
- 1 tablespoon olive oil
- 2 teaspoons sesame oil
- 1 pound baby bella mushrooms, sliced
- 12-ounce package fresh green beans
- 1 onion, sliced
- ¼ cup liquid amigos
- 1 tablespoon brown sugar substitute, like swerve brown sugar
- ¼ teaspoon white pepper
- 1 teaspoon rice wine vinegar
- 2 cloves garlic, minced
- ½ teaspoon ground ginger
- 1 teaspoon xanthan gum, to thicken if desired

Instructions
1. In a large skillet over medium-high heat, add the olive oil. Brown the chicken on both sides until cooked through (or almost cooked through). Remove from skillet and keep warm.
2. To the skillet, add the onions, green beans, and mushrooms. Cook, tossing occasionally while scraping the bottom of the skillet to remove any cooked pieces. Heat the vegetables until the mushrooms and onions are tender and the green beans are crisp-tender.
3. In a medium bowl, whisk together the remaining ingredients - except the xanthan gum - to create a sauce.
4. Add the chicken back to the skillet with the vegetables and pour the sauce over the top. Gently toss and continue to cook until the chicken is done.
5. To thicken the sauce, stir in the xanthan gum and allow it to simmer for 2 to 3 minutes. The sauce will continue to thicken after removed from heat.

Nutrition Information
Total Fat: 11g   Trans Fat: 0g   Carbohydrates: 8g
Carbohydrates: 3g Fiber: 5g Sugar: 0g Protein: 36g

18. Garlic Chicken With Zoodles

Prep Time: 15 Mins
Cook Time: 15 Mins
Total Time: 30 Mins

Ingredients
- 1 1/2 lbs boneless skinless chicken breasts
- 1 t olive oil
- 1 c low fat plain greek yogurt
- 1/2 c chicken broth
- 1/2 tsp garlic powder
- 1/2 tsp italian seasoning
- 1/4 c parmesan cheese
- 1 c spinach, chopped
- 3-6 slices sun-dried tomatoes
- 1 t chopped garlic
- 1 1/2 c zucchini cut into thin noodles

Instructions

How To Cook The Chicken
1. Heat the oil in a large skillet on medium.
2. Using paper towels, pat the chicken breast dry, sprinkle with salt and pepper for taste, and place in hot oil.

3. Cook on medium-high for 3-5 minutes on each side or until brown on each side and until no longer pink in center.
4. Remove chicken and set aside on a plate.
5. Add the yogurt, chicken broth, garlic powder, italian seasoning, and parmesan cheese into the large skillet.
6. Whisk over medium-high heat until it starts to thicken.
7. Add the spinach and sun-dried tomatoes.
8. Simmer until the spinach starts to wilt.
9. Add the chicken back to the pan and serve over zucchini noodles.

How To Cook The Zoodles
10. Preheat oven to 350 degrees f.
11. Using vegetable more spiral, cut zucchini into the shape of spiral noodles.
12. Place parchment paper on a large baking sheet. Spread and arrange zoodles and toss with sea salt. Be sure to spread them thin so they don't stick together.
13. Bake for 15 min for al dente. Add a couple of minutes if you want them softer.
14. Serve right away.

Nutrition Value
Carbohydrates: 8g   Protein: 60g   Fat: 15g   Saturated Fat: 4g   Cholesterol: 155mg   Sodium: 587mg   Potassium: 1122mg   Fiber: 1g   Sugar: 5g   Vitamin A: 1239iu   Vitamin C: 21mg   Calcium: 228mg   Iron: 2mg

19.	Skinny Chicken Salad

Total Time: 1 Hour 30 Mins
Ingredients
- 4 ounces shredded or diced (cooked) boneless, skinless, chicken breast (abt 1 cup)
- 1/4 cup diced celery
- 2 tablespoons sliced green onion
- 1/4 cup diced sweet, crisp apple
- 1 tablespoon light mayo
- 1 tablespoon light sour cream or greek yogurt
- Optional: 1/2-1 tablespoon chopped fresh parsley or cilantro
- 1/8 teaspoon curry powder
- 1/4 teaspoon red wine vinegar
- 1 tablespoon toasted sliced almonds
- Salt and pepper to taste

Instructions
1. Combine all ingredients except almonds and stir to combine. If possible, chill for an hour or so before eating.
2. Before serving, mix in almonds.
3. Eat-in a lettuce wrap, on whole-grain bread, in a wrap, or a pita.

Nutritional Info
Cal: 267g   Protein: 28g   Fat: 12g   Carbs: 8g   Fiber: 2g   Sugar:6 G

20.	Healthy Chicken Stir Fry

Prep Time: 15 Minutes
Cook Time: 15 Minutes
Total Time: 30 Minutes
Ingredients
For the marinade:
- 1/4 cup soy sauce, tamari, or coconut aminos
- 1 tablespoon lemon juice
- 1 tablespoon honey
- 1 tablespoon sesame oil
- 1 tablespoon rice wine vinegar

- 1/2 teaspoon red pepper flakes, plus more to taste for added heat
- 1 pound chicken breasts, cut into bite-sized pieces

For the stir fry:
- 3 cloves garlic, minced
- 3 large carrots, peeled and julienned
- 1 large red bell pepper, julienned
- 1 large yellow bell pepper, julienned
- 1 cup snow peas, sliced into 1" pieces
- 8 ounces button mushrooms, sliced thinly
- 2 cups frozen broccoli, defrosted
- 2 tablespoons avocado oil or olive oil, divided
- 1 tablespoon cornstarch or arrowroot powder
- 4 cups cooked rice, noodles, or other serving options
- Sliced green onions and toasted sesame seeds, for serving

Instructions

1. In a medium-sized bowl, whisk together the soy sauce, lemon juice, honey, sesame oil, rice wine vinegar, and red pepper flakes. Add in the chicken, and then toss to coat.
2. Let marinate in the fridge while you chop your veggies.
3. When you have all your veggies ready to go, heat a large wok over high heat. Add one tablespoon of olive oil.
4. Drain the chicken from the marinade, reserving the marinade, and placing it back in the fridge. Add the chicken to the wok and cook until the chicken is cooked for about five minutes. Remove the chicken to a plate.
5. Pour the remaining olive oil into the wok, and then add in the garlic.
6. Cook for a minute, or until fragrant. Add in the carrots, bell peppers, snow peas, and mushrooms.
7. Cook until bright in color and just crisp-cooked, about three minutes.
8. Add in the broccoli and cooked chicken. Reduce heat to medium-low.
9. Whisk the cornstarch into the reserved marinade, and then pour into the wok. Bring to a simmer and cook until thick, about five minutes.
10. Serve on top of rice or noodles, topped with green onions and toasted sesame seeds, and additional soy sauce, tamari, or coconut aminos, if desired.

Nutrition Information

Total Fat: 22g   Saturated Fat: 4g   Trans Fat: 0g
Unsaturated Fat: 17g   Cholesterol: 96mg   Sodium: 1312mg   Carbohydrates: 75g   Fiber: 11g   Sugar: 12g   Protein: 49g

21.	Green Chicken + Veggie Soup

Prep Time: 5 Mins
Cook Time: 25 Mins
Total Time: 30 Mins

Ingredients
- 1 tbsp. Extra virgin olive oil
- 1 small onion chopped
- 1 green bell pepper chopped
- 2 carrots chopped
- 2 stalks of celery chopped
- 3 cloves chopped garlic
- 1 tsp. Ground cumin
- 2 tsp. Dried oregano
- 12 ounces shredded chicken i like using a rotisserie
- 2 small zucchini chopped
- 1 cup frozen corn
- 6 cups low sodium chicken broth or homemade stock
- 1 bunch cilantro stemmed
- 1 serrano pepper
- A few handfuls of baby spinach chopped
- Salt and pepper to taste

Instructions

1. Heat olive oil in a large pot and add onions, pepper, carrots, and celery. Season with salt and pepper and cook for 8-10 minutes or until the veggies begin to look tender.
2. While veggies are cooking, blend cilantro, serrano pepper, 1 clove garlic, and 2 cups of broth in the blender. Set aside.
3. Once veggies are tender, season with cumin, oregano, and a little more salt and pepper, stir well and cook for another 2 minutes.

4. Add shredded chicken, zucchini, corn, remaining chicken broth, and the cilantro broth you blended in the blender. Bring to a boil, reduce down and simmer for 10 more minutes or until your veggies are tender.
5. Finish with a few handfuls of baby spinach and enjoy!

Nutrition
Calories: 301kcal   Protein: 43g   Fat: 12g   Saturated Fat: 2g   Cholesterol: 215mg   Sodium: 347mg   Potassium: 555mg   Vitamin A: 55iu   Calcium: 20mg   Iron: 1.8mg

22. Chicken Fajita Lettuce Wraps

Prep Time: 5 Mins
Cook Time: 25 Mins
Total Time: 30 Mins

Ingredients
- Lb chicken breast (thinly sliced into strips)
- Bell peppers (thinly sliced into strips)
- Tsp olive oil
- 2.0 tsp fajita seasoning
- Tbsp fresh lime juice
- 6.0 leaves romaine heart
- 1/4 cup non-fat greek yogurt (optional)

Instructions
1. Preheat. Preheat oven to 400°f
2. Combine. Combine all ingredients (except romaine) into a large plastic bag and seal. Mix well to evenly coat.
3. Prep. Empty the bag content onto a foil-lined baking sheet and bake 25-30 minutes until chicken is thoroughly cooked.
4. Serve. Serve on romaine leaves topped with greek yogurt (if desired).

Nutrition Value
Carbohydrates: 2.0g   Cholesterol: 80.0mg   Fat: 5.0g   Fiber: 2.0g   Protein: 40.0g   Sodium: 300.0mg   Sugar: 5.0g

23. Chicken And Green Beans

Prep Time: 10 Minutes
Cook Time: 20 Minutes
Total Time: 30 Minutes

Ingredients
- 1 tablespoon +1 teaspoon vegetable oil divided use
- 2 1/2 cups green beans trimmed and cut into 1-inch pieces
- 1 pound boneless skinless chicken breasts cut into 1 inch pieces
- 2 teaspoons minced garlic
- 1/4 cup low sodium chicken broth or water
- 1/4 cup soy sauce
- 3 tablespoons honey
- 2 teaspoons corn starch
- Salt and pepper to taste

Instructions
1. Heat 1 teaspoon of oil in a large pan over medium heat.
2. Add the green beans and cook for approximately 3-4 minutes or until beans are tender.
3. Remove the green beans from the pan; place them on a plate and cover.
4. Wipe the pan clean with a paper towel and turn the heat to high.
5. Add the remaining tablespoon of oil.
6. Season the chicken pieces with salt and pepper and add them to the pan in a single layer - you may need to

do this step in batches. Cook for 3-4 minutes on each side until golden brown and cooked through.
7. Add the garlic to the pan and cook for 30 seconds.
8. Add the green beans back to the pan and cook for 2 more minutes or until the green beans are warmed through.
9. In a bowl whisk together the chicken broth, honey, and soy sauce.
10. In a small bowl mix the cornstarch with a tablespoon of cold water.
11. Pour the soy sauce mixture over the chicken and green beans; cook for 30 seconds.
12. Whisk in the cornstarch and bring to a boil; cook for 1 more minute or until the sauce has just started to thicken, stirring constantly.
13. Serve immediately, with rice if desired.

Nutrition Value
Carbohydrates: 20g Protein: 27g Fat: 8g Cholesterol: 72mg Sodium: 651mg Potassium: 608mg Fiber: 1g Sugar: 15g Calcium: 37mg Iron: 1.5mg

24. 20 Minute Meal-Prep Chicken, Rice And Broccoli

Prep Time: 5 Minutes
Cook Time: 15 Minutes
Total Time: 20 Minutes

Ingredients
For rice:
- 2 cups water
- 1 cup jasmine rice
- 3/4 teaspoon salt

For The Chicken:
- 4 small-medium boneless skinless chicken breasts or thighs about 4 oz each
- 1 teaspoon brown or granulated sugar
- 1/2 teaspoon
- 1/2 teaspoon
- 1/2 teaspoon
- Salt and pepper to taste
- 1 tablespoon olive oil
- 2-3 cups broccoli florets
- Water for steaming

Instructions
1. To cook rice: bring the water to a boil in a medium saucepan. This stir in the rice; cover and reduce the heat to low. Simmer for 15 minutes until all of the water is absorbed.
2. To cook : rub chicken with brown sugar, paprika, cumin, garlic powder, salt, and pepper. Heat 1-2 tablespoons oil in a large heavy-duty pan or skillet over medium-high heat.
3. Add the chicken to the pan and cook for 5-6 minutes on the first side without moving, until the undersides develop dark grill marks.
4. Flip the chicken breasts using a pair of tongs or a fork and cook the other side for 5-6 minutes.
5. Turn off heat and allow chicken breasts to rest in the pan for at least 5 minutes before cutting.
6. To steam broccoli: there are two ways to cook broccoli. To blanch the broccoli on the stove-top. Boil water in a large pot. Add broccoli florets to pot and blanch for just 1 minute. Remove from the pot.
7. To steam in the microwave: place broccoli in a microwave-safe bowl and add water 3 tablespoons water to the bowl.
8. Cover with a ceramic plate or plastic wrap. Microwave on high for 3 minutes.
9. Cut the chicken into slices or small bite-size pieces.
10. Use a 1 cup measuring cup to evenly spoon 1 cup of rice into each (4 total) top the rice with slices of chicken and broccoli florets.
11. Cover and refrigerate for you to 4 days.
12. To reheat microwave on high for 2 minutes or until steaming.

Nutrition Value
Carbohydrates: 41g Protein: 26g Fat: 9g Saturated Fat: 2g Cholesterol: 107mg Sodium: 561mg Potassium: 474mg Fiber: 2g Sugar: 2g Vitamin A: 434iu Vitamin C: 41mg Calcium: 48mg Iron: 2mg .

25. Spinach Salad With Chicken And Farro

Prep Time: 10 Mins
Total Time: 10 Mins

Ingredients

- 1 cup uncooked bob's red mill farro
- 10 cups baby spinach or any baby greens
- 10 ounces thinly sliced leftover chicken breasts
- 2 cups shredded carrots
- 2 cups mushroom slices
- 2 cups red pepper slices
- Balsamic vinaigrette
- 6 tablespoons balsamic vinegar
- 3 tablespoons olive oil
- 1 tablespoon dijon mustard
- 1 teaspoon salt
- ½ teaspoon pepper

Instructions

1. Prepare farro according to package instructions and set aside to cool.
2. Place spinach in a large bowl or 5 individual travel containers. Top with chicken slices, carrots, mushrooms, red pepper slices and cooled farro.
3. In a small bowl, whisk together balsamic vinaigrette. Drizzle over salad bowl if you plan to serve immediately. Otherwise, place in a travel container and dress individual salads as needed throughout the week.

Nutrition Value

Carbohydrates: 50.8g   Protein: 25.5g   Fat: 11.8g
Saturated fat: 1.9g   Polyunsaturated fat: 9.9g
Cholesterol: 45mg Sodium: 841mg Fiber: 14.3g Sugar: 11.5g

26. One Skillet Italian Chicken

Prep Time: 10 Minutes
Cook Time: 20 Minutes
Total Time: 30 Minutes

Ingredients

- 2 large boneless, skinless chicken breasts sliced in half horizontally (about 1 ½ pounds)
- ¼ teaspoon salt
- ¼ teaspoon black pepper
- 1 tablespoon olive oil
- 1 small zucchini thinly sliced
- 1 medium bell pepper cored, seeded and thinly sliced
- 1 small yellow onion sliced
- 2 teaspoons minced fresh garlic
- 2 cups marinara sauce
- 1 (14.5 ounce) can diced tomatoes with juices
- 1 pinch crushed red pepper
- 1 ½ teaspoons italian seasoning
- 1 bay leaf
- 1 tablespoon chopped fresh parsley or basil (optional garnish)

Instructions

1. Season both sides of sliced chicken breasts with salt and pepper.
2. Heat oil in a large skillet over medium high heat. Add chicken and cook until golden brown, cooked through and no longer pink (about 4 minutes on each side depending on thickness). Transfer chicken to a plate and set aside (leave juices in skillet).
3. In the same skillet, cook zucchini, bell pepper and onion until zucchini is crisp-tender (about 3 to 4 minutes), stirring frequently.

4. Add garlic and cook an additional 30 seconds, while stirring.
5. Add marinara sauce, diced tomatoes, red pepper, italian seasoning and bay leaf. Stir to combine.
6. Bring to a simmer and simmer for 5 minutes, stirring occasionally (reduce heat as necessary to maintain a simmer).
7. Remove and discard bay leaf. Return chicken to skillet and coat with sauce mixture.
8. Serve sprinkled with chopped fresh parsley or basil, if desired.

Nutrition Facts
Calories: 298kcal carbohydrates: 16g protein: 40g fat: 9g saturated fat: 2g trans fat: 1g cholesterol: 109mg sodium: 1137mg potassium: 1417mg fiber: 5g sugar: 10g vitamin c: 67mg calcium: 84mg iron: 4mg

27. Chicken Pad Thai Recipe

Prep Time: 5 Minutes
Cook Time: 25 Minutes
Total Time: 30 Minutes

Ingredients
- 10 oz thai rice noodles
- 1 lb boneless skinless chicken breasts sliced into small strips
- 2 tbsp groundnut oil divided
- 1 red bell pepper sliced into thin strips
- 2 medium carrots peeled and cut into matchsticks
- 2-3 cloves garlic minced
- 2-3 green onions sliced into 1-inch pieces on diagonally
- 3 large eggs beaten
- ½ cup unsalted roasted peanuts chopped
- ⅓ cup cilantro chopped

Sauce
- ¼ cup maple syrup or honey
- ¼ cup light-sodium soy sauce or coconut aminos liquid
- 2 tbsp rice vinegar
- 1 lime juiced

Instructions
1. In a small bowl whisk all sauce ingredients. Set aside.
2. Cook the noodles according to package directions.
3. Heat 1 tbsp of the groundnut oil in a large skillet over medium heat. Add chicken and season with a pinch of salt and pepper.
4. Cook for 6-8 minutes, or until golden and cooked through. Set aside on a plate and cover to keep warm.
5. Add the remaining groundnut oil to the heated pan. Sauté the bell peppers together with carrots and garlic, stirring frequently, for 5-6 minutes. For the last minute, stir in the green onions.
6. Meanwhile, quickly beat the eggs in a small bowl.
7. Push the sautéed veggies to one side of the pan, and pour in the beaten eggs. Cook and scramble the eggs.
8. Return the cooked chicken to the pan, together with the noodles and the sauce.
9. Cook and toss over medium-low heat, until everything is combined and hot.
10. Take off the heat and sprinkle with chopped peanuts and fresh cilantro and enjoy!

Nutrition Value
Carbohydrates: 85g Protein: 38g Fat: 23g Saturated Fat: 4g Trans Fat: 1g Cholesterol: 195mg Sodium: 944mg Potassium: 909mg Fiber: 5g Sugar: 16g Vitamin C: 48mg Calcium: 106mg Iron: 3mg

28. Clean And Green Chicken Salad

Prep Time: 15 Minutes
Cook Time: 15 Minutes
Total Time: 30 Minutes

Ingredients
- 2 tbsp apple cider vinegar
- 2 tbsp olive oil, extra virgin
- 1 tsp thyme, dried
- 1 tsp granulated garlic
- 2 tsp sea salt, divided
- 2 tsp black pepper, divided
- 2 whole avocado
- 2 tbsp primal kitchen mayonnaise, or use 2 tbsp of my egg free cilantro avocado mayo
- 1 1/4 lb chicken breasts, boneless skinless
- 4 pieces celery
- 1 whole tomato, vine-ripened, chopped
- 1/4 cup kalamata olives
- 1 bunch cilantro, chopped
- 4 pieces butter lettuce, optional to make lettuce wraps

Process

For The Marinade
1. Mix apple cider vinegar, olive oil, dried thyme, dried garlic, and 1 tsp each of the sea salt and pepper into a bowl. Add chicken.
2. Let sit in the refrigerator at least 15 minutes, but it can marinade for up to 24 hours in a sealed container.

For The Salad
1. Mash diced avocado in a large bowl, and stir in mayo.
2. After chicken breasts have been in the marinade for at least 15 minutes, grill or bake until fully cooked. Let cool and chop.
3. Add chicken, celery, olives, herbs, tomato (option), salt and pepper to the avocado/mayo mixture. Stir to combine.
4. Eat as a salad or wrapped in butter lettuce leaves as a wrap.

Nutrirional Facts
Carbohydrates: 61g protein: 11g fat: 2g saturated fat: 0g cholesterol: 0mg sodium: 410mg potassium: 2224mg fiber: 11g sugar: 10g vitamin c: 196.8mg calcium: 358mg iron: 4.6mg

29. Chicken And Green Bean Stir Fry

Prep Time: 15 Minutes
Cook Time: 15 Minutes
Total Time: 30 Minutes

Ingredients
- 1/4 cup low sodium soy sauce or use gluten free soy sauce
- 1/2 cup chicken broth
- 1 tablespoon cornstarch
- 2 tablespoons mirin
- 1 tablespoon sugar
- 2 teaspoons sesame oil
- 1/4 teaspoon white pepper
- 1 tablespoon canola oil divided
- 1 tablespoon minced garlic
- 1 tablespoon minced ginger
- 1 pound chicken breast sliced very thinly
- 2 cups green beans
- Sesame seeds as garnish if desired

Instructions
1. In a large measuring cup or bowl add the soy sauce, chicken broth, cornstarch, mirin, sugar, sesame oil and

white pepper and whisk until everything is completely dissolved.
2. In a large skillet add one teaspoon canola oil on medium high heat and cook half the chicken until just cooked through, about 2-3 minutes on each side.
3. Repeat with the second half of the chicken and an additional teaspoon of oil.
4. Remove the chicken to a plate.
5. Add in the remaining oil, garlic and ginger and cook for 30-45 seconds until very fragrant but not browned.
6. Stir the garlic and ginger well and add in the sauce, whisking well.
7. Add in the green beans and let the sauce cook for 2-3 minutes until thickened.
8. Add in the chicken and stir well to coat.
9. Garnish with sesame seeds if desired.

Nutrition Information
Carbohydrates: 14.8g Protein: 26.9g Fat: 9.1g Saturated Fat: 0.8g Cholesterol: 75mg Sodium: 768mg Fiber: 1.5g Sugar: 6.3g

30.	All Green Chicken Fritters

Time To Make: 30 Mins
Ingredients
Fritters
- 1 cup grated courgette
- 1 quantity basic fritter mix (see tip)
- 7oz lean cooked chicken, diced
- 1 head broccoli, cut in florets, steamed and chopped
- 4 spears asparagus or 4oz green beans, steamed and chopped
- 2 cloves garlic, crushed
- 1 teaspoon dried mixed herbs
- 4 tablespoons fresh coriander or basil
- Spray oil

On The Side
- 2 cups cherry tomatoes
- 6 radishes, trimmed
- Spray oil
- 2 cups rocket
- ⅓ cup low-fat yoghurt
- 4 fresh coriander or basil leaves, chopped

Instructions
1. Combine half the courgettes and the rest of the fritter ingredients.
2. Heat oven to 360°f. Place tomatoes and radishes on baking tray, spray with oil and bake for 15 minutes.
3. Spray a non-stick pan with spray oil and place over a medium heat. Cook 2-3 fritters at a time, for 2-3 minutes each side or until golden brown.
4. Mix yoghurt and herbs together. Serve the fritters with roasted vegetables, remaining courgette, rocket and yoghurt on the side. Garnish with coriander or basil.

Nutrition Info
Protein 34g Total Fat 11g Saturated Fat 2g Carbohydrates 45g Sugars 10g Dietary Fibre 10g Sodium 390mg Calcium 300mg Iron 4mg

31.	Buffalo Chicken Pepper Nachos

Prep Time: 15 Minutes
Cook Time: 12 Minutes
Total Time: 27 Minutes

Ingredients
- 1 - 24 ounce bag mini sweet peppers
- 3 cups shredded cooked chicken
- 1/2 cup diced red onion

- 1/2 cup buffalo wing sauce + 2 tablespoons, divided
- 1 cup finely shredded sharp cheddar cheese
- 2 tablespoons ranch dressing
- 1/4 cup crumbled blue cheese
- 1 avocado, peeled and diced
- 2 tablespoons green onions

Instructions
1. Preheat the oven to 400 degrees. Spray a sheet pan with nonstick spray.
2. Cut the mini peppers in half and place face up on the prepared pan.
3. Mix together the chicken, onion, and 1/2 cup buffalo sauce in a bowl. Spoon the mixture evenly into the halved peppers.
4. Top the peppers with the cheese and bake for 12-14 minutes.
5. Remove the pan from the oven and drizzle with the ranch dressing and extra buffalo sauce.
6. Top with blue cheese crumbles, diced avocado, and green onions and serve immediately.

Nutrition Information
Total Fat: 22g   Saturated Fat: 9g   Trans Fat: 0g Unsaturated Fat: 11g   Cholesterol: 80mg   Sodium: 683mg Carbohydrates: 9g Fiber: 3g Sugar: 5g Protein: 21g

32.	**Green Chicken Chili**

Total Time: 15 Mins
Ingredients
- 1 lg white onion - diced
- 1 yellow bell pepper - diced
- 2 cloves garlic
- 1.5 lbs boneless skinless chicken thighs - cut into 1" pieces
- 1 16 oz jar salsa verde
- 1 15 oz can cannellini beans - rinsed and drained
- 1 32 oz box chicken stock
- Cheese, cilantro, jalapenos, onion, etc.. For garnish.

Instructions
1. In a large pot or dutch oven over medium high heat cook the onion, bell pepper and garlic in xvoo till softened and fragrant - about 3-5 minutes.
2. Add chicken, season with snp, and cook till chicken browns a bit - another 3-5 minutes.
3. Add remaining ingredients, bring to a boil and skim.
4. Cover pot, reduce heat to low and simmer for about an hour.
5. Garnish with cheese, jalapenos, onions and sour cream... Enjoy.

Nutritional Facts
Carbohydrates: 27g   Protein: 30g   Fat: 16g   Saturated Fat: 6g   Cholesterol: 18mg   Sodium: 163mg   Fiber: 6g Sugar: 5g Calcium: 103mg Iron: 4.6mg

33.	**Healthy Mongolian Chicken**

Prep Time: 5 Min
Cook Time: 15 Min
Total Time: 20 Min
Ingredients
- 3 tbsp. Low sodium soy sauce (gf if needed)
- 2 tbsp. Rice vinegar
- 2 tbsp. Hoisin sauce
- 2 garlic cloves, minced
- 1 tbsp. Ginger, minced (more to taste)
- 2 tsp. Sugar (leave out for low carb)

- 1 tsp. Cornstarch
- 1 tsp. Asian chili garlic paste (or sriracha or red pepper flakes)
- 1.33 lbs 99% lean ground chicken
- 12 green onions

Instructions
1. Mix together the soy sauce, hoisin, and rice vinegar.
2. Add in the garlic and ginger.
3. Add the sugar, cornstarch, and chili paste. Stir until smooth.
4. Heat the skillet over medium high heat. Spray with cooking spray. Add the chicken and cook for 5-7 minutes until cooked through, breaking it up as it cooks.
5. Add the green onions and sauce.
6. Cook for 3-4 minutes until sauce thickens and green onions are tender, stirring occasionally. Top with additional fresh green onions if desired.

Nutritional Facts
Total fat: 5g Saturated fat: 2g Cholesterol: 106mg Sodium: 783mg Total carbohydrate: 12g Dietary fiber: 2g Sugars: 6g Protein: 38g

34. Green Chicken Enchilada Cauliflower Casserole – Low Carb

Total Time: 30 Mins

Ingredients
- 20 oz frozen cauliflower florets (about 4 cups)
- 4 oz cream cheese, softened
- 2 cups cooked chicken, shredded
- 1/2 cup salsa verde
- 1/2 tsp kosher salt
- 1/8 tsp ground black pepper
- 1 cup shredded sharp cheddar cheese
- 1/4 cup sour cream
- 1 tbsp chopped fresh cilantro (optional)

Instructions
1. Put your cauliflower in a microwave safe dish and cook for 10-12 minutes or until fork-tender.
2. Add the cream cheese and microwave for another 30 seconds. Stir.
3. Add the chicken, salsa verde, salt, pepper, cheddar cheese, sour cream, and cilantro. Stir.
4. Bake in a preheated oven at 375 degrees (f) in an ovenproof casserole dish for 20 minutes.
5. Or you could microwave on high for 10 minutes.
6. Serve hot.

Nutrition Facts
Fat: 15g Carbohydrates: 3 g Fiber: 5 g Protein: 36g

35. Keto green bean and chicken stir fry

Prep Time: 5 Minutes
Cook Time: 15 Minutes
Total Time: 20 Minutes

Ingredients
- 1 pound boneless, skinless chicken breast, sliced thin
- ½ cup chicken broth
- 1 tablespoon olive oil
- 2 teaspoons sesame oil
- 1 pound baby bella mushrooms, sliced
- 12 ounce package fresh green beans
- 1 onion, sliced
- ¼ cup liquid aminos
- 1 tablespoon brown sugar substitute, like swerve brown sugar
- ¼ teaspoon white pepper

- 1 teaspoon rice wine vinegar
- 2 cloves garlic, minced
- ½ teaspoon ground ginger
- 1 teaspoon xanthan gum, to thicken if desired

Instructions

1. In a large skillet over medium-high heat, add the olive oil. Brown the chicken on both sides until cooked through (or almost cooked through). Remove from skillet and keep warm.
5. To the skillet, add the onions, green beans, and mushrooms. Cook, tossing occasionally while scraping the bottom of the skillet to remove any cooked on pieces. Heat the vegetables until the mushrooms and onions are tender and the green beans are crisp-tender.
6. In a medium bowl, whisk together the remaining ingredients except for the xanthan gum - to create a sauce.
7. Add the chicken back to the skillet with the vegetables and pour the sauce over the top. Gently toss and continue to cook until the chicken is done.
8. To thicken the sauce, stir in the xanthan gum and allow it to simmer for 2 to 3 minutes. The sauce will continue to thicken after removed from heat.

Nutrition Facts
Fat: 11g Carbohydrates: 8g Fiber: 5g Protein: 36g

36.	Chicken Soup With Greens

Prep Time: 5 Mins
Cook Time: 25 Mins
Total Time: 30 Mins

Ingredients
- 1 large onion diced
- 2 c carrot diced
- 3 c celery diced
- 4 cloves garlic finely chopped
- 1 teaspoon kosher salt
- ½ teaspoon pepper
- 2 teaspoons cinnamon
- 6 c chicken broth low sodium
- 10 large sprigs parsley plus extra for garnish
- 1 lb chicken breasts
- 1 bag spinach
- 15 oz can chick peas washed and drained
- ½ juice of a lemon or more to taste

Instructions

1. Saute onions, carrot and celery in a latch dutch oven or soup pot over medium heat for 5-7 minutes.
2. Add garlic, salt, pepper and cinnamon and continue cooking for additional minute.
3. Stir in chicken broth and whole parsley sprigs then bring to a boil.
4. Add raw, whole chicken breasts and bring to a simmer.
5. Cook for 10-12 minutes at a low boil.
6. Take one chicken breast out and cut in half to check for doneness.
7. When chicken is cooked through, remove and place on a cutting board to cool.
8. Begin shreddiing the chicken when it is cool enough to handle.
9. Add shredded chicken back into the broth and veggies.
10. Stir in spinach, chick peas and lemon juice.
11. Cook until spinach is tender, about 5 additional minutes.
12. Remove long parsley sprigs and garnish with fresh chopped parsley.

Nutrition Value
Calories: 308kcal Carbohydrates: 38.6g Protein: 36.4g
Fat: 3.5g Cholesterol: 60mg Sodium: 1654mg Fiber: 10.1g

37. Mexican Chicken Soup

Prep Time: 4 Mins
Cook Time: 26 Mins
Total Time: 30 Mins

Ingredients
- 8 cups chicken broth low sodium (or homemade)
- 1 medium onion quartered
- 1 teaspoon salt
- ½ teaspoon pepper
- 1 pound chicken breasts boneless, skinless
- 3 large carrots peeled and quartered
- Garnishes
- Lime juice
- Cilantro minced
- Avocado cubed
- Onion minced
- Jalapeno thinly sliced or minced

Instructions
1. Bring chicken broth, quartered onion, salt and pepper to a boil in a large soup pot. Add chicken breasts then bring back to a boil. Reduce to low and simmer for 20 minutes or until chicken breasts are cooked through.
2. Remove chicken from the pot and place on a cutting boar. Cut into large chunks then return to the broth. Add quartered carrots and cook until fork-tender, about 6-7 minutes.
3. Divide soup between four bowls then garnish with lime juice, cilantro, avocado, minced onion and jalapeño. Season with additional salt and pepper to taste.

Nutrition Value

Carbohydrates: 9g Protein: 26g Fat: 4g Saturated Fat: 0g Cholesterol: 72mg Sodium: 2471mg Potassium: 1008mg Fiber: 2g Sugar: 3g Vitamin A: 9055iu Vitamin C: 39.5mg Calcium: 58mg Iron: 1.6mg

38. Asian Chicken Cabbage Soup Recipe

Prep Time: 5 Mins
Cook Time: 15 Mins
Total Time: 20 Mins

Ingredients
- 2 teaspoons toasted sesame oil
- 1 tablespoon ginger minced
- 1 clove garlic minced
- Chili paste optional
- 4 cups chicken broth low sodium
- 2 tablespoons soy sauce low sodium
- 2 tablespoons rice vinegar
- 2 tablespoons hoisin sauce
- 1 cup cooked chicken breast shredded, such as rotisserie
- 2 cups cabbage shredded
- Salt and pepper to taste
- Cilantro, jalapeno slices optional garnish

Instructions
1. Heat sesame oil over medium heat in a stockpot. Add ginger, garlic and chili paste and saute until fragrant, about 30 seconds.
2. Pour in the chicken broth, soy sauce, rice vinegar, and hoisin sauce. Whisk to combine then increase heat to high.
3. Bring the pot to a boil then add in shredded chicken breast and cabbage. Reduce to low and simmer until cabbage is tender, about 5 minutes.

4. Season with salt and pepper to taste. Garnish with cilantro or jalapeño slices to serve.

Nutrition Value
Carbohydrates: 7g Protein: 13g Fat: 4g Cholesterol: 29mg Sodium: 1524mg Potassium: 365mg Fiber: 1g Sugar: 3g Vitamin A: 35iu Vitamin C: 29.5mg Calcium: 36mg Iron: 1.3mg

39. Greek Lemon Chicken Soup (Avgolemono)

Prep Time: 5 Mins
Cook Time: 20 Mins
Total Time: 25 Mins

Ingredients
- 6 cups chicken broth low sodium
- ¾ cups uncooked white rice
- ½ teaspoon salt
- ¼ teaspoon pepper
- 1 tablespoon cornstarch
- ¼ cup lemon juice about 1 lemon
- 2 eggs whisked a small bowl
- 8 ounces cooked chicken breast shredded – rotisserie works well
- Thinly sliced scallions optional garnish

Instructions
1. In a large soup pot, bring chicken broth to a boil. Add rice, salt and pepper and simmer until rice is tender, about 15 minutes.
2. Remove one cup of the broth from the pot and pour into a medium bowl. Add corn starch and whisk until dissolved. Pour in lemon juice and whisk once more.
3. To temper the eggs, slowly add the whisked eggs to the broth/cornstarch/lemon juice mixture. Whisk constantly so that the eggs gradually come to temperature. Continue until all of the eggs are fully incorporated.
4. Pour the warmed egg/broth mixture back into the large soup pot and stir until mixture begins to thicken, about 5 minutes.
5. Add shredded chicken breasts and cook until heated through. Check for seasoning and adjust accordingly. Serve with sliced scallions if you wish.

Nutrition Facts
Calories: 272kcal Carbohydrates: 30.7g Protein: 24.8g Fat: 4.4g Saturated Fat: 1.1g Polyunsaturated Fat: 3.3g Cholesterol: 135mg Sodium: 605mg Fiber: 0.4g Sugar: 1g

40. Instant Pot Chicken Curry (Green!)

Prep Time: 20 Minutes
Cook Time: 8 Minutes
Total Time: 28 Minutes
Servings: 6 Servings

Ingredients
- 1 ½ pounds boneless chicken thighs
- 1 small onion
- 1 red bell pepper
- 1 green bell pepper
- 2 small zucchini
- 3-4 cloves garlic minced
- 8-10 kaffir lime leaves
- 1 teaspoon coconut oil or vegetable oil
- 4 ounce green curry paste
- 2 tablespoon fish sauce
- 2 tablespoons palm sugar or 1 ½ tb brown sugar
- 14 ounces can coconut milk

- 1 cup canned bamboo shoots drained
- ½ cup Thai basil leaves or sweet basil
- 1 tablespoon cornstarch optional
- 1 tablespoon lime juice optional

Instructions

1. Prep work: Cut the chicken into 1-inch chunks. Peel the onion and remove the bell pepper seeds. Chop the onion, bell peppers, and zucchini into roughly 1-inch chunks. Keep them separate to add at different times. Mince the garlic. Crush the kaffir lime leaves in your hand to release the oils. Drain the bamboo shoots.
2. Set a large 6+ quart Instant Pot to Sauté. Add the coconut oil, chopped onions, minced garlic, and kaffir lime leaves. Sauté for 2 minutes to soften. Deglaze the bottom of the pot with ¼ cup water.
3. Add in the curry paste, fish sauce, palm sugar, and coconut milk. Stir well. Then mix in the chopped chicken.
4. Lock the lid into place. Set the Instant Pot on Pressure Cook High for 4 minutes. Once the timer goes off, perform a quick release. When the steam button drops it is safe to open the IP.
5. Set the IP back on Sauté. Stir in the bell peppers and bamboo shoots. Simmer for 2 minutes.
6. If the sauce seems thin, you can toss the zucchini chunks in 1 tablespoon of cornstarch to thicken the sauce. (This is often dependent on the thickness of the coconut milk and the moisture in the veggies.) Stir in the zucchini chunks. Simmer another 1-2 minutes. Then stir in the Thai basil.
7. Taste. Add fresh lime juice if desired. Serve with a side of white rice, cauliflower rice, or broccoli rice.

Nutrition

Calories: 488kcal, Carbohydrates: 18g, Protein: 23g, Fat: 37g, Saturatedfat: 20g, Cholesterol: 111mg, Sodium: 587mg, Potassium: 737mg, Fiber: 4g, Sugar: 11g, Vitamin A: 4543iu, Vitamin C: 69mg, Calcium: 72mg, Iron: 3mg

41. Perfect Baked Chicken Thighs

Prep Time: 5 Minutes
Cook Time: 25 Minutes
Total Time: 30 Minutes
Servings: 6

Ingredients

- 2 tablespoons olive oil
- 6 large, bone-in chicken thighs, or 8-10 small
- 3-5 sprigs of fresh thyme
- 3-5 sprigs of fresh rosemary
- 1 lemon, sliced into rounds
- 1/2 teaspoon garlic powder
- Salt and pepper

Instructions

1. Preheat the oven to 450 degrees F. Set a 12- to 14-inch cast-iron skillet on the stovetop over medium-high heat. Add the olive oil.
2. Pat the skin on the chicken thighs dry with paper towels. Sprinkle the thighs with garlic powder. Then sprinkle generously with salt and ground black pepper.
3. Once the oil is smoking hot, place the thighs in the skillet, skin side down. Sear for 5-7 minutes until the skin is golden-brown.
4. Flip the chicken thighs over and add the fresh herb sprigs and the lemon slices.
5. Place the entire skillet in the oven and roast for 15-18 minutes. Serve warm.

Nutrition

Calories: 290kcal, carbohydrates: 0g, protein: 18g, fat: 23g, saturatedfat: 5g, cholesterol: 110mg, sodium: 87mg, potassium: 231mg, fiber: 0g, sugar: 0g, vitamin a: 110iu, vitamin c: 2.1mg, calcium: 11mg, iron: 0.8mg

42. Thai Chicken Satay With Peanut Sauce

Prep Time: 24 Minutes
Cook Time: 6 Minutes
Total Time: 30 Minutes
Servings: 4

Ingredients
For The Chicken Satay:
- 1/2 pounds chicken tenders
- 1 cup unsweetened coconut milk
- tablespoons brown sugar
- tablespoons fish sauce
- 1 tablespoon ground coriander
- 1 teaspoon cumin
- 1/2 teaspoon turmeric
- 1 teaspoon salt
- Wooden Skewers, soaked
- For the Peanut Dipping Sauce:
- 1/2 cup peanut butter
- 1 tablespoon fresh minced ginger
- 1/3 cup chicken broth
- 1 tablespoon honey
- 1/4 cup low-sodium soy sauce
- tablespoons rice vinegar
- 3 tablespoons sesame oil
- 2 cloves garlic
- 1 tablespoon chile-garlic sauce, optional

Instructions
1. Combine the coconut milk, brown sugar, fish sauce, and spices in a large zip lock bag. Shake and add the chicken tenders. Marinate for at least 30 minutes.
2. Soak the skewers in water for at least 30 minutes.
3. Preheat the grill to direct medium heat. Weave each tender onto a skewer and lay it on a foil-covered cookie sheet.
4. Grill the Thai chicken satay for 3 minutes per side.
5. Meanwhile, puree all the ingredients for the peanut sauce in the blender and set aside.
6. Serve the chicken satay skewers over jasmine rice with spicy peanut sauce for dipping.

Nutrition
Calories: 690kcal, Carbohydrates: 25g, Protein: 47g, Fat: 46g, Saturatedfat: 18g, Cholesterol: 108mg, Sodium: 2458mg, Potassium: 1122mg, Fiber: 5g, Sugar: 16g, Vitamin A: 50iu, Vitamin C: 6.4mg, Calcium: 77mg, Iron: 3.7mg

43. Thai Cashew Chicken

Prep Time: 10 Minutes
Cook Time: 20 Minutes
Total Time: 30 Minutes
Servings: 4 Serving

Ingredients
- 4 tsp Luscious Lemon Oil or Roasted Garlic Oil or oil of your choice
- 1 1/2 lbs boneless, skinless chicken breast cut into thin strips
- 1 T or garlic, onion, lemongrass, salt, red bell pepper, black pepper, lime zest, and chiles
- 2 C green bell pepper, cut into thin strips
- 2 C red bell pepper, cut into thin strips
- 3 scallions sliced- separate whites and greens
- 24 cashews chopped into small pieces

Instructions
1. Heat oil in a large frying pan over medium-high heat.

2. Add chicken to the pan and cook for 3-5 minutes on each side until opaque.
3. Add peppers and whites of scallions to the pan and sprinkle with seasoning. Stir to combine.
4. Cover and cook over high heat for an additional 5-7 minutes, stirring occasionally until vegetables are crisp-tender and chicken is fully cooked.
5. Remove lid and sprinkle with nuts and scallion greens. Serve hot.

Nutrition
Calories: 323 Total Fat: 13.1g Sat Fat: 1.4g Cholesterol: 109mg Sodium: 92mg Carbohydrates: 12.3g Fiber: 2g Sugar: 6.6g Protein: 38.7g Calcium: 27mg Iron: 2mg Potassium: 919mg

44.	Ginger Lime Chicken And Noodles

Prep Time: 5 Minutes
Cook Time: 15-20 Minutes
Total Time: 25 (plus marinade time) Minutes
Servings: 4 Serving

Ingredients
- 4 tsp Valencia Orange Oil
- 1 Tablespoon Tasty Thai Seasoning (or garlic, lemongrass, lime, ginger, orange zest, red pepper, onion, salt, and pepper)
- Juice of one lime
- 1 1/2 lbs boneless, skinless chicken breasts (cut in half if large)
- 4 C prepared zucchini noodles

Instructions
1. Add the first three ingredients to a large zipper-style plastic bag.
2. Massage the plastic bag to combine the ingredients to make the marinade. Place chicken in the bag, squeeze out all the air, seal the bag, and store in the refrigerator for 4 hours, up to overnight.
3. When ready to cook the chicken, preheat outdoor grill (or indoor grill pan or frying pan). Cook chicken on both sides for 12-15 minutes over medium-high heat, until chicken is fully cooked. Verify temperature with a meat thermometer.
4. While chicken is cooking, prepare zucchini noodles. (Here's an easy recipe for zoodles)
5. Serve chicken over zoodles, or with your favorite side dish, and enjoy!

Nutrition
Calories: 252 Total Fat: 9g Sat Fat: 0.6g Cholesterol: 109mg Sodium: 98mg Carbohydrates: 3.8g Fiber: 1.2g Sugar: 2gProtein: 37.4g Calcium: 25mg Iron: 1mg Potassium: 925mg

45.	Cashew Chicken & Cauliflower Rice

Prep Time: 10 Minutes
Cook Time: 15-20 Minutes
Total Time: 30 Minutes
Servings: 4 Serving

Ingredients
- 4 tsp Valencia Orange Oil or unrefined coconut oil
- 3 scallions sliced into thin medallions
- 1 1/2 lbs boneless skinless chicken breast cut into a thin strip
- 1 C green bell pepper cut into thin strips
- 1 C red bell pepper cut into thin strips
- 2 C additional vegetables of your choice (broccoli, snow peas, zucchini, etc.)

- 1 T (or fresh garlic, chives, salt, pepper, onion, and parsley)
- 1/2 C low sodium chicken broth (if needed)
- 2 C prepared cauliflower rice
- 24 cashews, chopped into small pieces

Instructions
1. Add oil to a large frying pan over medium-high heat.
2. When hot, add scallion and cook for 1 minute until fragrant.
3. Add chicken and cook for 5-7 minutes until opaque.
4. Add all the vegetables and sprinkle with seasoning. If you are using thicker, heavier vegetables like broccoli, add the broth to help steam/cook them a little faster. Cover with a lid and allow to cook for 5 more minutes until veggies are crisp-tender, but not overdone.
5. While chicken is cooking, prepare cauliflower rice.
6. Remove chicken mixture from heat. Divide cauliflower rice into 4 equal portions. Do the same with the chicken mixture.
7. Place the chicken over the rice and sprinkle with 1/4 of the crushed cashews. Serve hot and enjoy!

Nutrition
Calories: 337 Total Fat: 13.2g Sat Fat: 1.4g Cholesterol: 109mg Sodium: 122mg Carbohydrates: 14.2g Fiber: 3.7g Sugar: 5.3g Protein: 40.8g Calcium: 69mg Iron: 2mg Potassium: 1111mg

46. Mediterranean Roasted Chicken With Lemon Dill Radishes

Prep Time: 5 Minutes
Cook Time: 25 Minutes
Total Time: 30 Minutes
Servings: 4 Serving

Ingredients
- 2 lbs chicken thighs (Remove skin if on Lean & Green. If using bone-in chicken, add additional cooking time)
- Pinch of Desperation Seasoning (or garlic, salt, black pepper, onion, and parsley)
- 1 Tablespoon
- Mediterranean Seasoning (or garlic, marjoram, basil, rosemary, and onion)

Instructions
1. Preheat oven (or outdoor BBQ Grill) to 375 degrees.
2. Season the chicken with just a pinch of Dash of Desperation Seasoning
3. Place the chicken in a baking dish large enough to hold them without touching one another (this speeds up the cooking process.)
4. Sprinkle chicken with Mediterranean seasoning.
5. Bake in preheated oven for 25 minutes, or until chicken reaches 175 degrees F.
6. Remove from oven and serve hot, or chilled over greens for a salad.

Nutrition
Calories: 269 Total Fat: 10.5g Sat Fat: 2.9g Cholesterol: 12mg Sodium: 122mg Carbohydrates: 0g Fiber: 0g Sugar: 0g Protein: 41g Calcium: 21mg Iron: 2mg Potassium: 344mg

47. Chicken With Garlic And Spring Onion Cream

Prep Time: 10 Minutes
Cook Time: 20 Minutes
Total Time: 30 Minutes
Servings: 4 Serving

Ingredients

- Nonstick cooking spray
- 1 1/2 lbs boneless, skinless chicken breasts, pounded to 3/8" thickness
- 1 teaspoons Dash of Desperation Seasoning (or natural sea salt and black pepper)
- 1 C low sodium chicken broth
- 2 teaspoons fresh lemon juice
- 1 Tablespoon (1 capful)
- Garlic and Spring Onion Seasoning (or fresh garlic, chives, salt, pepper, and lemon)
- 4 Tablespoons low-fat cream cheese
- 2 Tablespoons butter
- Fresh basil, parsley, and/or lemon wedges for garnish if desired

Instructions
1. Pound chicken into 3/8" thickness. The easiest way to do this is to place one breast in a large plastic bag and hit it with the back of a small frying pan. Be careful to do this on a cutting board, or another safe surface. You do not want to crack your countertops!
2. Spray a large, nonstick pan with cooking spray and place the pan over medium-high heat.
3. Season each chicken breast with a pinch of Dash of Desperation Seasoning. When the pan is hot, place chicken in the pan.
4. Cook chicken for 5-7 minutes on one side then flip to the other side. Cook an additional 5 minutes more.
5. Add the broth, lemon juice, and Garlic and Spring Onion to the pan. Stir well to combine. Using a spatula, scrape all the yummy brown bits off the bottom of the pan.
6. Let the mixture come to a simmer and continue to cook for 10-12 minutes until the sauce is reduced to only about 1/3 of a cup.
7. Add the cream cheese and butter to the pan and whisk to combine.
8. Remove from stove and sprinkle with fresh basil or other herbs and fresh lemon wedges or slices if desired. Serve hot with your favorite side dish.

Nutrition
Calories: 285 Total Fat: 13.5g Sat Fat: 5.9g Cholesterol: 135mg Sodium: 158mg Carbohydrates: 1.3g Fiber: 0.1g Sugar: 0.1g Protein: 37.1g Calcium: 23mg Iron: 1mg Potassium: 657mg

48. Creamy Skillet Chicken And Asparagus

Prep Time: 10 Minutes
Cook Time: 15 Minutes
Total Time: 25 Minutes
Servings: 4 Serving

Ingredients
- 4 teaspoons Stacey Hawkins Roasted Garlic Oil (or oil of your choice and fresh garlic)
- 1 3/4 lbs boneless, skinless chicken breast, cut into 1" chunks
- 1/2 C low sodium chicken broth
- 1 Tablespoon (one capful) Stacey Hawkins Garlic and Spring Onion or Garlic Gusto Seasoning or fresh chopped garlic, parsley, and chives
- 8 T (4 oz or half an 8 oz block) light cream cheese
- 4 C fresh asparagus, cut into 2" pieces
- Pinch of salt and pepper and garlic)

Instructions
1. Add oil to a large skillet and heat over medium-high heat.
2. When hot, add chicken breasts and cook for 7-10 minutes, stirring occasionally. The chicken should be slightly browned.
3. Pour the broth into the pan and, using a spatula, scrape all the browned bits (fond) off the bottom of the pan.
4. Add garlic seasoning, cream cheese, and asparagus. Turn the heat to high.
5. Stir the ingredients continually, allowing the cream cheese to melt evenly into the sauce. Bring to a boil and simmer until a thick, rich sauce has formed. Divide into 4 equal portions, sprinkle with a little Dash of Desperation and serve hot.

Nutrition

Calories: 302 Total Fat: 12.8g Sat Fat: 3.5g Cholesterol: 114mg Sodium: 223mg Carbohydrates: 7.1g Fiber: 2.8g Sugar: 4.4g Protein: 39g Calcium: 134mg Iron: mg Potassium: 851mg

49. Toasted Sesame Ginger Chicken

Prep Time: 10 Minutes
Cook Time: 15 Minutes
Total Time: 25 Minutes
Servings: 4 Serving

Ingredients
- 4 teaspoons oil of your choice and orange zest
- 1 1/2 lbs boneless, skinless chicken breast
- 1 Tablespoon of toasted sesame seeds, garlic, onion powder, red pepper, ground ginger, salt, pepper, and lemon

Instructions
1. Place chicken breasts on a clean, dry cutting board.
2. Using a meat mallet or backside of a frying pan, gently flatten the chicken breasts to approx. 3/8" thickness.
3. Sprinkle with seasoning.
4. Heat Valencia Orange Oil in a large, nonstick frying pan over medium-high heat.
5. Add chicken and cook for 7-8 minutes on one side, until a lovely crust has formed- it will be slightly brown.
6. Gently flip chicken and cook on the other side for an additional 5-6 minutes until the chicken is fully cooked.
7. Serve warm with your favorite side dish, or chilled over salad. Makes about 4 servings.

Nutrition

Calories: 247 Total Fat: 9.9g Sat Fat: 0.8g Cholesterol: 109mg Sodium: 87mg Carbohydrates: 0.5g Fiber: 0.3g Sugar: 0g Protein: 36.5g Calcium: 30mg Iron: 1mg Potassium: 640mg Calcium: 0mg Iron: 0mg Potassium: 130mg

50. Pan Seared Balsamic Chicken And Vegetables

Prep Time: 5 Minutes
Cook Time: 25 Minutes
Total Time: 25 plus marinade time Minutes
Servings: 4 Serving

Ingredients
- 1 1/2 pounds boneless, skinless chicken thighs
- 1Tablespoon (one Capful) of salt, pepper, garlic, red pepper, parsley, garlic powder, and onion to taste
- 4Tablespoon of balsamic reduction
- 1Tablespoon Dijon Mustard
- 2 C cherry or grape tomatoes, halved
- 2 C zucchini sliced into 3/8" slices (try to have the zucchini around 1" in diameter- smaller ones cook faster and have fewer seeds)
- 1/3 C water

Instructions
1. Whisk together balsamic, mustard and seasoning in a bowl large enough to hold the chicken.
2. Add the chicken and toss to coat. Place in the refrigerator for 20 minutes, up to 8 hours to marinate.
3. When ready to cook, preheat the oven to 425 degrees.

4. Place a well-seasoned cast-iron skillet (large enough to hold all the chicken without crowding) over medium-high heat.
5. Shake off the excess marinade (reserving it in the bowl for later) and place the chicken in the pan. Cook until seared and slightly browned for about 5 minutes. Flip chicken and cook an additional 5 minutes on the other side.
6. While chicken is cooking, prepare the vegetables.
7. Add water to the remaining marinade in the bowl and whisk to combine.
8. Scatter the vegetables around the pan. Season with a pinch of salt and pepper.
9. Pour the marinade mixture over the veggies & chicken. Toss to combine. Place in the preheated oven for 15 minutes additional.
10. Remove from oven and serve hot.

Nutrition
Calories: 280 Total Fat: 9.9g Sat Fat: 2.7g Cholesterol: 114mg Sodium: 179mg Carbohydrates: 7.5g Fiber: 1.9g Sugar: 5g Protein: 38.7g Calcium: 42g Iron: 2mg Potassium: 690mg

51.	Surf And Turk Burgers

Prep Time: 5 Minutes
Cook Time: 20 Minutes
Total Time: 25 Minutes
Servings: 4 Serving

Ingredients
- 1 1/4 pounds (20 oz) ground turkey
- 8 medium raw shrimp, peeled, deveined and tails removed (each shrimp should be about 1 oz each)
- 1 Tablespoon of garlic, lemon, parsley, onion, salt, pepper, and celery

Instructions
1. Preheat the outdoor grill to 350 degrees.
2. Place the turkey in a large bowl, sprinkle with seasoning and using your hands, combine well.
3. Form turkey mixture into 4 individual patties.
4. Gently press two raw shrimp into the top of the burger in a heart shape.
5. Place on the grill and cook for 5-7 minutes on both sides until done. Turkey must be an internal temperature of 165 degrees F.
6. Remove from the grill and serve with a great side dish!

Nutrition
Calories: 191 Total Fat: 9.7g Sat Fat: 1.7g Cholesterol: 132mg Sodium: 216mg Carbohydrates: 0.3g Fiber: 0g Sugar: 0g Protein: 28.1g Calcium: 41mg Iron: 2mg Potassium: 266mg

52.	Tex Mex Turkey Stuffed Poblanos

Prep Time: 10 Minutes
Cook Time: 20 Minutes
Total Time: 30 Minutes
Servings: 4 Serving

Ingredients
- 2 large poblano peppers (or bell peppers) cut in half lengthwise and seeds removed
- 4 tsp (or fresh garlic and oil of your choice)
- 2 pounds ground turkey, 98% lean
- 1 T (one capful) or Phoenix Sunrise Seasoning (or garlic, onion, cilantro, cumin, and black pepper)

- 1 C reduced-fat extra sharp cheddar cheese, shredded (divided)
- 8 T sour cream
- Fresh cilantro and/or sliced jalapenos for garnish

Instructions
1. Preheat the oven to 350 degrees. Spray a casserole dish large enough to hold the pepper halves with nonstick cooking spray and place the peppers, cut side up into the dish. Bake for 15 minutes.
2. While peppers are cooking, add the Roasted Garlic Oil to a large skillet and heat over medium-high heat.
3. Add turkey to the pan and sprinkle with the seasoning. Cook for 10 minutes, stirring occasionally until turkey is browned.
4. Remove meat from the heat and stir in 1/2 C of the cheddar cheese.
5. Remove the peppers from the oven and place equal portions of the meat into the pepper halves. Sprinkle with remaining cheese and bake until poblanos are tender and cheese is melted for about 5-7 additional minutes.
6. Drizzle 2 T of sour cream over each pepper and sprinkle with cilantro and/or jalapenos if desired.

Nutrition
Calories: 357 Total Fat: 14.4g Sat Fat: 7.3g Cholesterol: 140mg Sodium: 324mg Carbohydrates: 4.1g Fiber: 0.3g Sugar: 1.2g Protein: 55g Calcium: 397mg Iron: 2mg Potassium: 705mg

53. Lean Green Chicken Soup

Prep Time: 15 Minutes
Cook Time: 25 Minutes
Total Time: 40 Minutes

Servings: 12

Ingredients
- 2 quarts chicken broth or stock
- 1 1/2 pounds boneless, skinless chicken breast
- 2 celery stalks, chopped
- 2 cups green beans, cut into 1-inch pieces
- 1 1/2 cups peas, fresh or frozen
- 2 cups asparagus, cut into 1-inch pieces, tops, and middles (avoid tough ends)
- 1 cup diced green onions
- 4-6 cloves garlic, minced
- 2 cups fresh spinach leaves, chopped and packed
- 1 bunch watercress, chopped with large stems removed
- 1/2 cup fresh parsley leaves, chopped
- 1/3 cup fresh basil leaves, chopped
- 1 teaspoon salt
- 1/2 teaspoon ground black pepper

Instructions
1. Pour the chicken broth into a large pot, and set over medium-high heat. Add the chicken breasts and bring to a simmer. Cook for 15 minutes.
2. Add the celery, green beans, peas, asparagus, onions, garlic, salt, and pepper. Simmer for 5-10 minutes until tender, then remove from heat.
3. Remove the chicken breasts and shred with two forks or chop into bite-sized pieces. Return to the pot.
4. Stir in the spinach, watercress, parsley, and basil. Taste, then salt and pepper as needed.

Nutrition
Calories: 105kcal, Carbohydrates: 7g, Protein: 15g, Fat: 2g, Saturated Fat: 0g, Cholesterol: 36mg, Sodium: 852mg, Potassium: 556mg, Fiber: 2g, Sugar: 2g, Vitamin A: 1345iu, Vitamin C: 30.3mg, Calcium: 52mg, Iron: 1.9mg

VEGETARIAN RECIPES

54. 10 Minute Lean & Green Tofu Stir-Fry

Cook Time: 10 Mins
Total Time: 10 Mins

Ingredients
- 1/4 cup chopped onion
- 1/4 cup chopped button mushrooms
- 8 oz extra-firm tofu, pressed and chopped into bite-size cubes
- 3 teaspoons nutritional yeast
- 1 teaspoon braggs liquid aminos or coconut aminos
- 4 cups baby spinach
- 4–5 grape tomatoes, chopped
- Cooking spray

Instructions

1. Spray a non-stick skillet with cooking spray and heat over medium heat. Add onion and mushrooms and sauté until onions are translucent and mushrooms have softened (about 2-3 minutes).
2. Add tofu to the skillet. Toss to combine and cook for 1-2 minutes more.
3. Add your nutritional yeast and liquid aminos to the pan. Stir until everything is well coated.
4. Add spinach and tomatoes. Cook for 3-4 minutes longer, until spinach, is starting to wilt a tiny bit. Plate, top with sriracha, and serve.

Nutrition Value
Sugar: 2g Fat: 11g Carbohydrates: 7g Fiber: 5g Protein: 18g

55. Calabacitas Recipe (Con Queso)

Prep Time: 15 Minutes
Cook Time: 10 Minutes
Total Time: 25 Minutes
Servings: 6

Ingredients
- 4 tablespoons butter, or oil
- 1 small sweet onion, peeled and chopped
- 3 cloves garlic, minced
- 2-3 corn cobs, corn cut off the cob
- 1-2 zucchini, cut into ½ inch cubes
- 1-2 yellow squash, cut into ½ inch cubes
- 1 large poblano pepper, seeded and chopped
- 1 red bell pepper, seeded and chopped
- 1 orange bell pepper, seeded and chopped
- ¼ cup chopped cilantro
- ½ lime, juiced
- 1 teaspoon ground cumin
- 1 teaspoon dried oregano
- Salt and pepper

Instructions

1. Set an extra-large cast iron cast over medium-high heat. Add the butter, onion, garlic, and poblano pepper. Saute and soften for 3-5 minutes, stirring occasionally.
2. Add the ground cumin and oregano to the skillet. Stir and push the onions to the sides of the skillet.
3. Add about a third of the chopped squash and bell peppers. Brown for 1 minute. Then push them to the sides of the pan and add another third of the veggies. Cook for 1 more minute. Then push the veggies to the sides and add the remaining squash and peppers.

4. Season with 1 teaspoon salt and ¼ teaspoon ground black pepper. Brown another minute, then stir in the corn, cilantro, and juice of ½ a lime.
5. Stir to warm the corn, then turn off the heat. The veggies should be just barely cooked and still firm.
6. Serve warm with a generous sprinkling of crumbled queso fresco, a dollop of pico de gallo, avocado slices, and extra lime wedges.

Nutrition
Calories: 222kcal, carbohydrates: 23g, protein: 7g, fat: 13g, saturatedfat: 8g, cholesterol: 34mg, sodium: 501mg, potassium: 474mg, fiber: 3g, sugar: 12g, vitamin c: 87mg, calcium: 153mg, iron: 1mg

56. Heavenly Green Beans And Garlic

Prep Time: 5 Minutes
Cook Time: 10 Minutes
Total Time: 15 Minutes
Servings: 4 Serving

Ingredients
- 1 1/2 pounds green beans (about 4 cups) ends trimmed
- 1/2 capful (1/2 Tablespoon) fresh chopped garlic, salt, and pepper
- 1Tablespoon of other fat of your choice
- 4 Tablespoons freshly grated Parmesan cheese

Instructions
1. Place green beans in a pot with a lid and add 1" of water to the bottom.
2. Sprinkle seasoning over the top of the beans, trying to keep most of the seasoning on the beans and out of the water.
3. Place the covered pot on the stove over high heat. Bring water to a boil and let the beans steam for 5-7 minutes, until bright green and crisp-tender. Be careful not to overcook.
4. Carefully drain all the water out of the pot.
5. Drizzle with Roasted Garlic Oil and a pinch of salt and pepper (or Dash of Desperation Seasoning for more pop!) Sprinkle with cheese and serve hot.

Nutrition
Calories: 84 Total Fat: 5g Sat Fat: 1.5g Cholesterol: 5mg Sodium: 127mg Carbohydrates: 7.8g Fiber: 3.7g Sugar: 1.5g Protein: 4g Calcium: 81mg Iron: 1mg Potassium: 230mg

57. Roasted Garlic Zoodles

Prep Time: 5 Minutes
Cook Time: 5 Minutes
Total Time: 10 Minutes
Servings: 4 Serving

Ingredients
- 1Tablespoon Garlic Oil) or other fat of your choice
- 6 Cups zucchini noodles
- 1/2 capful (1/2 Tablespoon) of fresh chopped garlic, salt, and pepper
- Pinch of salt and pepper or Dash of Desperation Seasoning to taste

Instructions
1. Add the oil/spray to a larger sized frying pan and heat over medium-high heat.
2. Add the zucchini noodles to the pan and sprinkle with seasoning.
3. Cook for just 2-3 minutes, tossing occasionally with a pair of tongs.
4. Season with a pinch of salt and pepper (or Dash of Desperation Seasoning for more pop!) and serve hot.

Nutrition
Calories: 57 Total Fat: 3.7g Sat Fat: 0.5g Cholesterol: 0mg Sodium: 17mg Carbohydrates: 5.7g Fiber: 1.9g Sugar: 2.9g Protein: 2.1g Calcium: 25mg Iron: 1mg Potassium: 444mg

58. Healthy Baked Zucchini Fritters

Prep Time: 5 Mins
Cook Time: 15 Mins
Total Time: 20 Mins

Ingredients
- 2 medium zucchini /courgettes
- 2 eggs
- Zest of 1 lemon
- A bunch of basil leaves chopped
- 2 spring onions finely chopped
- ½ cup wholewheat/plain.gluten-free flour
- ½ tsp baking powder
- Salt and pepper to taste
- Spray oil

Instructions
1. Preheat oven to 200c/400f.
2. Grate zucchini and sprinkle with a pinch of salt, then transfer in a clean kitchen cloth and make sure to squeeze out their excess liquid.
3. In a large bowl mix together grated zucchini, lemon zest, eggs, basil leaves, spring onion and flour. Season generously with salt and pepper.
4. Fold in baking powder and quickly stir all together.
5. Lightly spray with oil a mini muffin tin and pour 1 tbsp of the mixture in each mould.
6. Bake for 10 mins, then turn the fritters on the other side and bake for a further 5 mins or until crispy and golden brown.
7. Serve with lemon wedges and homemade mayo.

Nutrition
Calories: 296 Total Fat: 4.8g Cholesterol: 38mg Sodium: 80mg Carbohydrates: 0.4g Sugar: 0.2g

59. Wild Garlic Soup

Prep Time: 15 Minutes
Cooking Time: 30 Minutes

Ingredients
- 1 onion, chopped
- 1 tbsp rapeseed oil
- 250g new potatoes, scrubbed and cubed
- 125g wild garlic leaves, washed and roughly chopped
- 1 litre vegetable stock or 1 litre water with 1 tsp vegetable bouillon
- Squirt of lemon
- Salt
- Mild chilli flakes

Instructions
1. In a large saucepan, sauté the onion in the rapeseed oil for about 10 minutes, until soft, add the cubed potatoes and quickly stir-fry.
2. Add the stock to the onion and potatoes. Simmer until the potatoes are just soft, which will take 15 minutes, depending on the size of the cubes of potato.
3. Add the wild garlic, cover and simmer for a couple of minutes until cooked, but are still a vibrant green color. Either serve at once chunky or liquidise to a smooth consistency.

4. Check for seasoning and add a squirt of lemon juice. Decorate with mild chilli flakes. Serve hot.

Nutrition: per serving
Calories 291kcal Fat 17.8g (10.8g saturated) Protein 3.7g Carbohydrates 16.4g (3.8g sugar) Fibre 3.3g Salt 1g

60.	Salsa Verde With Capers

Prep Time: 15 Minutes
Ingredients
- 2 garlic cloves, peeled
- 2 tbsp capers
- 25g fresh mint leaves
- 25g fresh basil leaves
- 1 tsp apple juice concentrate
- 1 tbsp lemon juice
- 100ml extra virgin olive oil

Instructions
1. Put everything in the food processor in the above order buzzing each time before adding next ingredient.
2. The mix should be a dip consistency, add more olive oil if too thick.
3. Serve cold as a dip, as a salad dressing, with asparagus, mix in with pasta, enliven rice dishes or drizzle over roasted vegetables.

Nutrition Facts
Calories: 172kcal Carbohydrates: 2g Protein: 1g Fat: 18g Saturated Fat: 3g Cholesterol: 2mg Sodium: 77mg Potassium: 112mg Fiber: 1g Sugar: 1g Vitamin A: 1617IU Vitamin C: 21mg Calcium: 36mg Iron: 1mg

61.	Forager's Nettle Pesto

Total Time: 30 Mins
Ingredients
- 100g young stinging-nettle leaves
- 100 ml good olive oil
- 2-3 garlic cloves, chopped finely
- 2 tsp mild red chilli, chopped finely (or dried chilli flakes)
- 1 tsp black pepper, freshly ground
- 50g hazel nuts (or sunflower kernels)
- Juice of 1 lemon

Instructions
1. Put the nettle leaves into a bowl and cover with cling film and microwave on full power for 2 minutes.
2. Take out of the microwave, leave the cling film on and allow to cool for 5 minutes.
3. Alternatively, cover and steam the nettle leaves for 5 minutes until tender.
4. Fry the chilli in 2 teaspoons of the olive oil until soft and the oil is coloured.
5. In a food processor add the rest of olive oil, the fried chilli, and all the chopped garlic and blitz.
6. Add the nettle leaves and combine to a smooth purée.
7. Add black pepper and lemon juice to taste.
8. Heat the hazel nuts in a dry frying pan over a moderate heat, stirring or tossing them, until they just start to colour.
9. Careful or they will burn.
10. Immediately tip into a bowl to cool. Coarsely crush in a mortar and pestle.
11. With a spatula, remove the nettle purée from the food processor bowl into a serving bowl. Add the hazel nuts and gently mix in.

Nutrition Facts
Calories: 96kcal Carbohydrates: 4g Protein: 5g Fat: 7g Saturated 4g Cholesterol: 18mg Sodium: 107mg Potassium: 36mg Sugar: 1g

62. Winter Coleslaw With Barberries

Total Time: 30 Minutes

Ingredients
- 300-400g mixed cabbage - white, green or red
- A few brussels sprouts, shredded
- 1 medium carrot, peeled and grated
- 1 small parsnip, peeled and grated
- 1/4 small celeriac, peeled and grated
- 1 small beetroot, peeled and grated
- 1 small red onion, peeled and sliced
- Handful of parsley, large stalks removed
- Handful of mint leaves
- Handful of dried barberries, soaked, drained and rinsed
- Handful of sunflower seeds, toasted
- Handful of pumpkin seeds, toasted

Dressing
- 2-3 tbsp olive oil
- 1 lemon or lime
- Sea salt

Instructions
1. Finely shred the cabbages and brussels sprouts by hand or using the slicer attachment of a food processor and place into a large mixing bowl.
2. Add the grated carrot, parsnip, celeriac and beetroot.
3. Finely slice the red onion and place into a small bowl of cold water, making sure it is fully submerged. This will help to remove the strong pungency of the onion flavour, and crisp up the texture.
4. Chop the fresh herbs roughly, and add to the grated vegetables.
5. To make the dressing, squeeze the lemon or lime and mix the juice with the olive oil and red chilli if using. Taste and add enough agave syrup to slightly sweeten.
6. Drain the onion in a sieve, then add to the other vegetables.
7. Pour over the dressing and mix thoroughly through the coleslaw.
8. Season with a pinch of salt and taste. Add a little more salt, oil or lemon if necessary.
9. Sprinkle over the barberries, sunflower and pumpkin seeds.
10. This coleslaw will keep for up to 3 days in a container in the fridge.

Nutrition Facts
Calories: 106kcal Carbohydrates: 5g Protein: 6g Fat 4g Saturated 3g Cholesterol: 19mg Sodium: 96mg Potassium: 26mg Sugar: 2g

63. Lingonberry Sauce

Prep time: 10 minutes
Cook time: 10 minutes

Ingredients
- 10g freeze-dried lingonberries
- 100ml water
- 20g golden caster sugar
- 2 star anise

Instructions
1. Place all the ingredients into a small saucepan and bring to a gentle simmer.

2. Simmer for 5 minutes or until the lingonberries have rehydrated and the sugar is dissolved and the sauce has thickened, and then take off the heat and leave to infuse.
3. Remove the star anise before serving.
4. Can be served warm or cold.

Nutrition Facts
Calories70 cal Total Fat0g Total Carbohydrate18g Dietary Fiber1g Sugars18g Added Sugars18g Protein 0g

64. Ackee Stir-Fry

Prep Time: 15 Minutes
Cook Time: 5 Minutes

Ingredients
- 1 tin ackee (340g drained weight)
- 250g green beans, trimmed
- 1 red pepper, sliced
- 1 orange pepper, sliced
- 1 bunch spring onions, sliced
- 1 tbsp jerk spice paste
- 1 tbsp water
- 1-2 habanero chilli, de-seeded and sliced
- 1 tsp jerk spice mix

Instructions
1. Drain the ackee and rinse.
2. Trim the tops off the green beans. Finely slice the peppers and spring onion.
3. Heat a large wok. Fry the jerk spice paste for a few seconds. Add the pepper and green beans, adding splashes of water to help create steam to cook the vegetables.
4. Stir-fry for a few minutes until the vegetables are tender but still with a bite to them. Add the ackee, sliced chilli and spring onion and stir-fry for a further minute, sprinkle with jerk spice mix.
5. Serve with plain rice

Nutrition Facts
Calories: 151; Fat: 0; Protein: 2.9 to 8.9 grams;

65. Healthy Cream Of Broccoli Soup

Prep Time: 10 Minutes
Cook Time: 20 Minutes
Total Time: 30 Minutes

Ingredients
- 3 cup roughly chopped broccoli
- 1 cup grated carrot
- 1/4 cup cashew cream
- 2 tbsp all purpose flour
- 1 tbsp avocado oil
- 2-3 cloves small garlic minced
- 1 cup almond milk (or regular milk if not vegan)
- 2 cup water (or vegetable stock)
- Salt and pepper

Instructions
1. Heat oil on a low heat in a medium pan.
2. Add garlic and sauté for a few seconds or until fragrant. Then add the flour and cook for about 2 min. Continuously stir it to avoid browning.
3. Slowly add milk and water with continuous stirring. Take care not form lumps. Bring the mixture to a boil.
4. Now add broccoli, grated carrots, salt and pepper. Cook the mixture for about 15-18 mins.
5. Add cashew cream, mix well and cook for another 2-3 min.
6. Turn off the heat and serve warm to enjoy this bowl of deliciousness.

Nutrition Value
Calories: 150kcal, Carbohydrates: 14g, Protein: 10.5g, Fat: 7g, Saturated Fat: 4g, Cholesterol: 19.5mg, Sodium: 796.5mg, Fiber: 4g, Sugar: 6.5g

66.	Chipotle Guacamole Deviled Eggs

Prep Time: 5 Mins
Cook Time: 11 Mins
Total Time: 16 Mins

Ingredients
- 6 large eggs
- 2 medium avocados
- 1 tsp finely chopped chipotle
- ½ red onion finely chopped
- ¼ cup chopped cilantro;
- 2 tbsp fresh lemon or lime juice;
- Salt and pepper to taste.

Instructions
1. In a pot of boiling water, fold in the eggs and allow to cook for 11 min.
2. In the meantime, prepare the guacamole. cut the avocado in half and scoop out the flesh.
3. Put avocados and the remaining ingredients into a blender and mix until creamy, season to taste with salt and pepper.
4. Pour the guacamole into a piping bag and refrigerate until ready to use.
5. When the eggs are ready, cool them under cold running water, and peel them.
6. Cut each egg horizontally in half and scoop out the cooked yolks. You can use them for another recipe or in salads.
7. Pipe the guacamole into each egg half, season to taste and serve.

Nutrition Value
160 Calories Total Fat: 13g Cholesterol: 220mg Sodium: 200mg Total Carbohydrates: 3g Dietary Fiber: 0g Total Sugars: 2g Protein: 7g

67.	The Easiest Vegan Pad Thai

Prep Time: 15 Mins
Cook Time: 15 Mins
Total Time: 30 Mins

Ingredients
- 200 gr flat rice noodles
- 1 garlic clove finely minced
- 1 red chilli finely sliced
- 60 gr snow peas
- 100 gr sprouting broccoli
- 4 baby corns roughly chopped
- 100 gr red cabbage finely chopped
- 1 large carrot peeled and julienned
- 50 g dry roasted peanuts roughly chopped
- Juice of 1 lime
- 2 spring onions finely chopped
- Handful of fresh cilantro leaves finely chopped

For The Sauce:
- 60 ml gluten-free soy sauce or tamari or fish sauce for non vegan version
- 1 tbsp tamarind paste thinned with 2 tsp of water
- 2 tbsp brown sugar
- A pinch of red pepper flakes

Instructions
1. Soak the noodles in lukewarm water for 6-7 min. Then drain and rinse under cool water and set aside in a colander.
2. In a small bowl, combine together soy sauce, tamarind, sugar, and red pepper flakes.
3. Heat a large wok over medium heat. Swirl a glug of olive oil in the pan, add in garlic and chilli and stir fry for a few seconds. Remove them from the pan and set aside.
4. Add into the pan sprouting broccoli, snow peas, baby corn, carrots and red cabbage and stir-fry for a 3-4 minutes.
5. Stir in the noodles and sauce and combine with the rest of the ingredients. Add in the garlic and chilli previously set aside and stir-fry for 1-2 minutes, then remove from the pan.
6. Squeeze the juice of a lime over the noodles, then sprinkle the spring onion, cilantro and roasted peanuts on top and serve.
7. Store in an airtight container in the fridge for up to 2 days.

Nutrition Value
Calories: 347kcal   Carbohydrates: 64g   Protein: 9g   Fat: 7g   Saturated Fat: 1g   Sodium: 1044mg   Potassium: 375mg   Fiber: 4g   Sugar: 13g   Vitamin A: 3632iu   Vitamin C: 65mg   Calcium: 71mg   Iron: 2mg

68.	The Best Vegan Pesto Recipe

Cook Time: 5 Minutes
Total Time: 5 Minutes
Ingredients
- 2 cups or 140 g fresh basil leaves
- 2/3 cup or 90 g raw macadamia nuts
- 2 cloves garlic
- 2 tablespoons nutritional yeast
- 3 tablespoons extra virgin olive oil
- 3-4 tablespoons water
- Sea salt and freshly ground black pepper, to taste

Instructions
1. Add basil leaves, macadamia, garlic and nutritional yeast in a cup of a food processor or blender and blend until a thick paste forms, scrapping sides.
2. Add extra virgin olive oil and water, one tablespoon at a time, until smooth.
3. Add sea salt and freshly ground black pepper to taste.
4. Enjoy!

Nutrition Value
Calories: 209kcal   Carbohydrates: 5g   Protein: 4g   Fat: 20g   Saturated Fat: 3g   Sodium: 3mg   Potassium: 284mg   Fiber: 3g   Sugar: 1g   Vitamin A: 3120iu   Vitamin C: 11.1mg   Calcium: 123mg   Iron: 2.7mg

69.	Kale Pesto With Cashew And Parmesan

Total Time: 5 Minutes
Ingredients
- 1 bundle kale chopped, stalks removed (about 3 cups)
- 1/2 cup cashew nuts toasted
- 2/3 teaspoon salt or less if you use parmesan
- 1/2 teaspoon black pepper
- 3 cloves garlic
- 1/3 cup grated parmesan cheese omit or use hard vegan cheeses if vegan or vegetarian
- 1 cup olive oil

Instructions

1. Using a food processor or an immersion blender, pulse chopped kale, toasted cashew nuts, salt, black pepper, garlic and parmesan cheese (if using) until smooth.
2. Gradually add oil until you like the consistency.
3. Add more oil or more cashew nuts to adjust the consistency.
4. Serve with pasta, bread, salads, sandwiches, potatoes, roasted or fresh vegetables, eggs, fish, soups, beans or anything else you like.
5. Enjoy!

Nutrition Value
Calories: 91kcal   Carbohydrates: 3g   Protein: 3g   Fat: 7g   Saturated Fat: 1g   Cholesterol: 3mg   Sodium: 261mg   Potassium: 97mg   Vitamin A: 750iu   Vitamin C: 8.9mg   Calcium: 62mg   Iron: 0.7mg

70. Vegan Broccoli Pesto Pasta

Prep Time: 5 Mins
Cook Time: 10 Mins
Total Time: 15 Mins

Ingredients
- 350 gr (about 1 head) broccoli florets
- 350 gr short pasta (i use paccheri)
- Handful fresh basil leaves
- 60 gr toasted pine nuts
- 1 garlic clove, grated
- Zest of 1 lemon
- 1 tsp fresh lemon juice
- 60 ml extra-virgin olive oil
- Sea salt & freshly cracked black pepper

To Serve:
- Toasted pine nuts
- Handful of basil leaves
- Lemon zest
- Freshly cracked black pepper

Instructions
1. Cook the broccoli florets in a large pot of lightly salted boiling water, for about 5 minutes, or just until tender.
2. With the help of a slotted spoon, transfer the florets from the water into a bowl with cold water and ice, then drain and set aside.
3. Fold the pasta into the pot used for cooking the broccoli and cook until al dente, about 10 minutes for paccheri.
4. Add broccoli florets, basil leaves, pine nuts, garlic, lemon juice and zest into a food processor and pulse until crumbly.
5. Set the food processor on slow speed and gently pour in the extra-virgin olive oil. Continue to mix until your broccoli pesto reaches a creamy texture.
6. Add 60 ml (¼ cup) of pasta cooking water into the broccoli pesto and continue to mix until reaching a creamy texture. Season with sea salt and black pepper to taste.
7. Drain the pasta, return to the pot and stir in the broccoli pesto.
8. Divide the broccoli pesto pasta among 4 plates, top with extra pine nuts, lemon zest, basil leaves and freshy cracked black pepper, and serve

Nutrition Value
Calories: 589kcal   Carbohydrates: 73g   Protein: 16g   Fat: 27g   Saturated Fat: 3g   Sodium: 35mg   Potassium: 561mg   Fiber: 6g   Sugar: 4g   Vitamin A: 545iu   Vitamin C: 79mg   Calcium: 60mg   Iron: 3mg

| 71. | Vegan Zuppa Toscana |

Prep Time: 10 Minutes
Cook Time: 20 Minutes
Total Time: 30 Minutes

Ingredients
- 1 tablespoon olive oil
- 1 yellow onion diced
- 3-4 medium yukon gold or russet potatoes peeled and diced
- ½ cup sun-dried tomatoes in oil drained and finely chopped
- 1 tsp dried oregano
- 5 sprigs fresh thyme
- 4 cups vegetable stock
- 2 cups almond milk unsweetened
- 3 cups kale leaves ribs removed, chopped
- 1 14 oz can cannellini beans
- 1 tablespoon nutritional yeast
- ¼ cup fresh parsley chopped
- 1 tablespoon lemon juice
- ½ tsp red pepper flakes or to taste optional
- Salt and pepper to taste
- 1 teaspoon vegan pesto per portion to serve
- Crusty bread to serve

Instructions
1. Preheat a large heavy bottom pot over medium heat. Add the olive oil and onion and sautée for a few minutes until translucent.
2. Add diced potatoes and continue cooking for 2-3 minutes, stirring often.
3. Add sun-dried tomatoes, minced garlic, oregano and thyme and sautée for one more minute.
4. Scrape all the brown bits from the bottom of the pan.
5. Add vegetable stock and bring to a boil. Cook for about 7 minutes, until the potatoes are softened. Add unsweetened almond milk and bring to a boil.
6. Add kale and cook for 5 minutes.
7. Add cannellini beans, nutritional yeast, parsley and lemon juice (if using).
8. Sprinkle with chili flakes (optional), salt and pepper to taste. Serve with a dollop of vegan pesto and crusty bread on the side. Enjoy!

| 72. | Pumpkin And Kale With Creamy Polenta |

Total Time: 30 Minutes

Ingredients
For Pumpkin And Kale With Creamy Polenta:
- 250 grams or 1 1/2 cup polenta
- 1 l or 4 1/2 cups water
- 50 grams or 1/2 cup grated parmesan optional
- 1/2 small pumpkin
- 1 small red chili pepper
- 4 sprigs fresh thyme
- Vegetable oil
- 1 clove garlic chopped
- 200 grams or 7 oz curly kale chopped, veins removed
- 1/3 leek sliced
- Black pepper
- Salt
- 120 grams or 4 oz mozzarella optional

For The Dressing:
- 5 tablespoons olive oil
- 2 teaspoons balsamic vinegar
- 1 teaspoon lemon juice

- 1 teaspoon demerara sugar optional
- 2 tablespoons freshly chopped basil
- Black pepper
- Salt
- 4 tablespoons pomegranate seeds to serve

Instructions

1. In a pot, bring water with a tablespoon of salt to a boil. Gradually add polenta, cover with a lid and reduce the heat to low. Cook for 10 minutes, stirring frequently. Remove from the heat, add parmesan (optional),cover and let rest for 15 minutes.
2. Meanwhile, slice the pumpkin. Heat a lug of vegetable oil in a large pan or wok over medium high heat. Add pumpkin and cook until the pumpkin it is soft, about 8 minutes. Chop red chili pepper and thyme leaves and add them before the pumpkin is ready. Transfer to a plate and put the pan or wok back on the stove.
3. Add a bit of oil to the pan and once it's hot, add garlic and kale. Add a pinch of salt and black pepper and cook until soft, about 4 minutes. Transfer to a plate.
4. Add leek slices and cook until soft and slightly golden, about 4 minutes.
5. Make the dressing: combine olive oil, balsamic vinegar, lemon juice, demerara sugar (optional), chopped basil, a pinch of salt and black pepper. Arrange polenta, pumpkin, kale and leek on two plates. Add sliced mozzarella (optional). Serve with balsamic dressing and pomegranate seeds. Enjoy!

Nutrition Value

Calories: 684kcal   Carbohydrates: 83g   Protein: 18g   Fat: 21g   Sodium: 25mg   Potassium: 661mg

73. The Best Vegan Corn Chowder

Prep Time: 10 Minutes
Cook Time: 20 Minutes
Total Time: 30 Minutes

Ingredients

- 1 tablespoon olive oil
- 1 medium-sized onion, chopped
- 3 ears grilled corn on the cob (or fresh sweet corn, husked)
- 2 cloves garlic, minced
- 2-3 small yellow potatoes, diced
- 1 zucchini, diced
- 1 yellow bell pepper, diced
- 700 ml or 3 cups homemade vegetable broth
- 1 400 ml or 14 oz can light coconut milk
- 1 tablespoon white wine vinegar
- 1 teaspoon smoked paprika
- Pinch of salt
- 1/2 teaspoon freshly ground black pepper
- 5 tablespoons millet
- 4 tablespoons avocado dill dressing, optional
- 4 sprigs fresh dill, to garnish

Instructions

1. In a large pot, heat a lug of olive oil and sauté your onions until translucent. Slice kernels off the corn. Add garlic, diced potatoes, zucchini and bell pepper, corn kernels (saving 4 tablespoons for garnishing), and continue sautéing for about 5 more minutes, stirring occasionally.
2. Add vegetable broth, coconut milk, vinegar, smoked paprika, salt, freshly ground black pepper and millet.

3. Cover and simmer for 10-15 more minutes, until the potatoes are done.
4. If it's too thick to your taste, thin it up with a bit more vegetable broth.
5. Pulse half the soup in a blender until smooth and return it back to the pot.
6. Stir everything well and serve with avocado dill dressing, corn kernels and fresh dill. Enjoy!

Nutrition Value
Calories: 205kcal Carbohydrates: 35g Protein: 6g Fat: 4g Sodium: 719mg Potassium: 718mg Fiber: 6g Sugar: 5g Vitamin A: 1650iu Vitamin C: 61.4mg Calcium: 49mg Iron: 4.5mg

74.	Cauldron Curry

Total Time: 10 Mins

Ingredients

Curry paste:
- 1 tbsp. Whole coriander seeds
- 2 tsp. Whole cumin seeds
- 1 tsp. Whole black peppercorns
- 1 tsp. Coarse salt
- 3 serrano chiles
- 1/2 c. Fresh cilantro
- 2 stalk fresh lemongrass
- 8 clove garlic
- 2 scallions
- 2 tbsp. Chopped peeled fresh ginger
- 2 tbsp. Fresh lime juice
- 1 tbsp. Finely grated lime zest

Stew:
- 2 oz. Spinach
- 1 can unsweetened regular coconut milk
- 1 can unsweetened light coconut milk
- 1 medium zucchini
- 12 oz. Boneless, skinless chicken breasts
- 12 oz. Boneless, skinless chicken thighs
- Coarse salt and freshly ground pepper
- 3/4 c. Fresh basil
- Serrano chiles
- Squeamish squash with rice
- Lime wedges

Instructions
1. **Make the curry paste:** grind coriander, cumin, peppercorns, and salt with a mortar and pestle, or with the bottom of a heavy skillet.
2. Add remaining ingredients, and grind until a paste forms.
3. **Make the stew:** puree 5 tablespoons curry paste, the spinach, and 1 cup regular coconut milk in a blender until smooth.
4. Reserve remaining curry paste for another use.
5. Bring remaining regular coconut milk and the light coconut milk to a boil in a medium dutch oven or heavy stockpot.
6. Reduce heat, stir in curry-spinach mixture, and simmer for 5 minutes.
7. Add zucchini, and cook until slightly tender, about 5 minutes.
8. Add chicken, and season with salt and pepper. Cook until zucchini is tender and chicken is cooked through, about 5 minutes.
9. Add basil, and garnish with serrano chiles.
10. Serve with squeamish squash with rice and lime wedges.

Nutrition Facts
Protein: 32.1g Carbohydrates: 27.7g Dietary Fiber: 2.3g Sugars: 6.4g Fat: 9.4g Calcium: 66.4mg Iron: 1.8mg Magnesium: 59.7mg Potassium: 792.8mg Sodium: 360mg.

75. Vegan Zucchini Quinoa Sushi Rolls

Prep Time: 15 Mins
Total Time: 15 Mins

Ingredients
- 1 cup cooked quinoa
- 2 small-medium zucchini
- 1 carrot cut into strips
- 1 avocado cut into strips
- A bunch of fresh mint leaves chopped
- Light soya sauce to serve
- Wasabi to serve

Instructions
1. Cover with cling film a bamboo sheet. In the meantime, cut the zucchini lengthwise into very thin strips with the help of a peeler.
2. Arrange the thin zucchini slices slightly overlapping each other, carrying on until you have a long strip enough to make 4 rolls out of it.
3. Consider a couple of extra cm per side, as the edges will be chopped off to ensure all rolls are even.
4. Place ½ cup of quinoa on top, press a thin layer of quinoa onto the bottom. Make sure you have a even layer that covers horizontally half the zucchini bed.
5. Arrange carrots and avocado into a long even strip on top of quinoa.
6. Start to roll up, making sure to keep the roll tight, and gently pressing down with your fingers all the way until you reach the end. Be careful not to squeeze out the roll filling.
7. Once the roll is ready, you can cover in cling film and refrigerate for 15 mins to firm it up. Or you can use a sharp knife and carefully cut it into 4 even rolls, chopping the two ends off.
8. Serve accompanied by soy sauce and wasabi, or refrigerate for up to 3 hours and serve later.

Nutrition Facts
Calories: 327kcal Carbohydrates: 6g Protein: 11g Fat: 29g Saturated Fat: 13g Cholesterol: 77mg Sodium: 888mg Potassium: 470mg Fiber: 1g Sugar: 1g

76. Green Shakshuka

Prep Time: 5 Mins
Cook Time: 20 Mins
Total Time: 25 Mins

Ingredients
- 1 tbsp olive oil
- ½ cup leek approx ⅓ - ½ of a leek, diced
- ½ green pepper small, cut in long slices
- 3 ½ oz eggplant 100g, diced
- 3 oz kale 85g, weight without stems, roughly chopped
- 2 tbsp cilantro/coriander roughly chopped
- 2 ½ tbsp parsley roughly chopped, divided
- ¼ cup cream 4tbsp/60ml, suggest heavy/double
- 1 egg
- 2 oz feta cheese 55g, cut into small cubes or broken up

Instructions
1. Warm the oil in a small skillet/frying pan and add the diced leek. Cook for a minute then add the peppers and eggplant. Cook, stirring now and then, until the vegetables are all fairly soft - around 5mins - but not brown.
2. Add the kale to the pan and stir it in so that it wilts. Add the cilantro, 2tbsp parsley and cream, stir it all so it is well mixed and heat a minute so the cream starts to simmer.

3. Create a slight well in the middle and crack your egg into the well. Scatter the feta over the top and cover the pan with a lid. Leave a couple minutes until the egg white cooks but only just as the egg will continue to cook after you takes it off the heat.
4. Serve with the remaining parsley over the top (or a little more, as you prefer), suggested with bread on the side.

Nutrition Facts
Carbohydrates: 27g Protein: 20g Fat: 53g Saturated Fat: 25g Cholesterol: 295mg Sodium: 768mg Potassium: 987mg Fiber: 5g Sugar: 9g

77. Hummus With Basil Cilantro Oil

Prep Time: 15 Minutes
Total Time: 15 Minutes

Ingredients
For Hummus
- 2 15- oz. Cans chick peas garbanzo beans, rinsed and drained
- 1 1/2 teaspoons kosher salt
- 1/2 cup tahini well stirred
- 2 lemons zested and juiced
- 1 tablespoon garlic chopped
- 1/2 teaspoon cumin
- 1/2 cup olive oil
- 5 -6 tablespoons warm water

For Basil Cilantro Oil
- 1 cup basil leaves
- 1 cup cilantro leaves and stems
- 1 large clove garlic roughly chopped
- 1/2 jalapeno seeds and membrane removed, roughly chopped
- 1/2 cup olive oil

Instructions
For Hummus
1. Combine the chick peas, lemon zest, lemon juice, kosher salt and garlic in the bowl of a food processor. Pulse until finely chopped.
2. Add the tahini and cumin and pulse until combined. In a steady stream add the olive oil while the processor is running.
3. Add water a tablespoon at a time, pulsing after each addition, until you achieve the desired consistency.

For The Basil Oil
1. Combine the basil, cilantro, garlic and jalapeno in a blender and mix until roughly chopped.
2. With the blender running on low speed, add the oil in a steady stream.
3. When the oil is combined, turn the blender up incrementally until the herbs etc.
4. Have been pureed in the oil.
5. Spoon hummus into a serving dish.
6. Swirl a spoon in the hummus, creating divots and valleys.
7. Pour several tablespoons of the herbed oil over the hummus.
8. Serve with pita chips and your favorite vegetables for scooping.

Nutrition Facts
Calories: 194kcal Carbohydrates: 10g Protein: 3g Fat: 16g Saturated Fat: 2g Sodium: 199mg Potassium: 133mg Fiber: 2g Sugar: 1g

78. Spring Pesto Green Beans

Prep Time: 5 Minutes
Cook Time: 5 Minutes
Total Time: 10 Minutes

Ingredients
- 1 pound green beans trimmed
- 1/2 teaspoon kosher salt
- 2 tablespoons pesto sauce preferably homemade
- 2 tablespoons sliced almonds
- Sprinkle shaved parmesan

Instructions
1. Toast the almonds
2. Preheat the oven to 400°. Lay the almonds on a baking sheet in a single layer.
3. Bake for 5-7 minutes until lightly browned and fragrant.

For Warm Beans:
1. Bring a medium saucepan of water to a boil.
2. Add the kosher salt and green beans.
3. Cook the beans until they are crisp tender, about 3-5 minutes.
4. Drain the beans well and add the pesto.
5. Use tongs to toss the beans in the pesto until well coated.
6. Transfer the beans to a serving bowl and sprinkle with toasted almonds and shaved parmesan.
7. Serve.

Nutrition Value
Calories: 92kcal   Carbohydrates: 9g   Protein: 3g   Fat: 5g   Sodium: 367mg   Potassium: 274mg   Fiber: 3g   Sugar: 4g

79. Pesto Zucchini Noodles Shrimps & Feta

Prep Time: 5 Mins
Cook Time: 7 Mins
Total Time: 12 Mins

Ingredients
- 3 medium large zucchini
- A glug of extravirgin olive oil
- 200 gr fresh king prawns/shrimps cleaned and deveined
- 100 gr cherry tomatoes halved
- 3 tbsphomemade pesto
- 100 gr feta cheese
- A bunch of fresh basil leaves
- Zest of ½ lemon
- Sea salt and freshly cracked black pepper

Instructions
1. With the help of a spiralizer or julienne peeler, make zucchini noodles.
2. Fold the zucchini noodles in a large pot of lightly salted boiling water and cook for 1-2 mins.
3. In the meantime, heat a large pan with a glug of olive oil. Stir in the shrimps and cherry tomatoes and cook for about 3-4 mins, until the prawns are cooked through. Season to taste with sea salt and black pepper.
4. Drain the zoodles and add fold them into the pan with the other ingredients. Mix in the pesto and remove from the heat.
5. Scatter crumbled feta and basil leaves all over, and top with grated lemon zest. Serve immediately.

80. Baked Beet Falafel Vegan Quinoa Bowl

Prep Time: 10 Minutes
Cook Time: 20 Minutes
Chilling Time: 30 Minutes
Total Time: 30 Minutes

Ingredients
- ½ Cup (100 grams) dry chickpeas soaked overnight then drained
- 1 large beet peeled and coarsely grated (about 1 ½ cup)
- 1/2 medium onion coarsely chopped
- 5 cloves of garlic roughly chopped, divided
- 1 tablespoon ground cumin
- 2 teaspoons coriander
- 1 ½ tablespoons flour
- 2 teaspoons sea salt divided
- Pepper To Taste
- ½ cup (75 grams) raw cashews soaked overnight or in hot water for 15 minutes
- ½ cup (120 ml) unsweetened plant milk
- 2 tablespoons lemon juice
- 2 ½ tablespoons fresh dill
- 2 ½ tablespoons horseradish
- 1 cup (200 grams) quinoa
- A bunch (125 grams / 4.5 oz) of asparagus tough ends snapped off and cut in half
- 1 cucumber sliced
- 1 avocado sliced
- 4 radishes sliced
- A small bag of mixed salad greens
- 25 cherry tomatoes halved

Instructions

1. Squeeze some of the water out of the beet then pulse the chickpeas, beet, onion, 4 cloves of the garlic, cumin, coriander, flour, 1 ½ teaspoons of the salt and pepper in a food processor until you have a rough, course meal that's not quite a paste. Place in the fridge for at least 30 minutes.
2. Meanwhile, prepare the sauce by blending the cashews, milk, lemon juice, dill, horseradish, remaining clove of garlic and remaining ½ teaspoon of sea salt until creamy. Put in the fridge to thicken and allow the flavours to blend.
3. Prepare the quinoa according to the package directions. Blanch the asparagus in boiling water for just a couple of minutes until bright green. Refresh in cold water to stop the cooking process. Set aside.
4. Preheat the oven to 200°c (400°f) and line a baking pan with parchment paper or foil.
5. Form the falafel into balls, squeezing out some of the juice into a separate bowl. If they're not sticking together, you can either put the mix back into the food processor and process a bit more or add more flour, a tablespoon at a time, until they hold together. Bake for 20 minutes or until the balls are crispy and browned on the outside. Allow to cool for a couple of minutes before carefully peeling them off the pan.
6. Make the bowls by dividing the quinoa between four bowls and topping with the vegetables and beet falafel. Serve the sauce on the side to drizzle over.

Nutrition Value
Calories: 507kcal   Carbohydrates: 68g   Protein: 18g
Fat: 20g   Saturated Fat: 2g   Sodium: 1270mg
Potassium: 1391mg   Fiber: 14g   Sugar: 11g

81. Spring Vegetable Zoodle Pasta

Prep Time: 5 Minutes
Cook Time: 10 Minutes
Total Time: 15 Minutes

Ingredients
- 75 grams (2.6 oz) whole wheat spaghetti
- 1 bunch (125 grams / 4.5 oz) asparagus tough ends snapped off and cut into pieces
- 25 snow peas sliced into two pieces on the diagonal
- 2 tablespoons olive oil
- 3 big cloves of garlic grated with a microplane or pressed
- 6 radishes thinly sliced
- ½ teaspoon sea salt
- The juice and zest of half a lemon
- ½ tablespoon of the pasta water
- 1 medium zucchini spiralized and cut into short-ish pieces or julienned or thinly sliced with a veg peeler
- Pepper to taste

Instructions
1. Cook the pasta according to the package directions. Drain, reserving half a tablespoon of the cooking water.
2. In the meantime, bring a small pot of water to the boil and blanch the asparagus spears for a couple of minutes until crisp-tender. Transfer to a bowlful of cold water to stop the cooking process. Then blanch the snow peas until crisp-tender and also transfer to cold water. Drain.
3. Heat a large pan over medium heat. Add the oil and garlic. Fry, stirring often, until the garlic is golden. Remove from the heat and add the pasta, asparagus, peas, radishes, salt, lemon juice, pasta water, zoodles and pepper. Toss well to coat everything in the garlicy oil.
4. Serve and sprinkle with lemon zest.

Nutrition Value
Calories: 305kcal Carbohydrates: 38g Protein: 9g Fat: 15g Saturated Fat: 2g Sodium: 600mg Potassium: 570mg Fiber: 3g Sugar: 5g

82. Vegan Potato Leek Soup

Prep Time: 5 Minutes
Cook Time: 25 Minutest
Otal Time: 30 Minutes

Ingredients
- 4 medium-sized leeks
- 1 large potato
- 1 ½ cups vegetable stock
- ½ cup (75 grams) raw cashews soaked overnight or in hot water for 15 minutes
- ½ cup (120 ml) water
- 1 head of garlic
- 1/8 teaspoon olive oil
- ½ teaspoon lemon juice
- ½ teaspoon salt to taste (depends how salty your stock is. Mine was pretty salty so i didn't add any more salt)
- The seeds of half a pomegranate optional
- A few herb leaves of your choice - mint, basil, cilantro, chives, etc.

Instructions
1. Heat a saucepan over medium heat and add a couple tablespoons of water.
2. Slice the white and light green parts of the leeks. The more green you add, the more off-white your soup will

be so it's up to you how much green to use. Add the leeks to the pan and sweat for about 5 minutes.
3. Peel and dice the potato and add it to the pan. Sweat for another couple of minutes then add 1 cup of the vegetable stock, reduce the heat to medium-low and partially cover the pan. Cook for 20 minutes, or until the vegetables are very soft and falling apart.
4. Cut the top off the head of garlic, drizzle over 1/8 teaspoon of oil and microwave "roast" it on high for 2 minutes or until soft. You can use a garlic roaster or place it on a plate and cover with a lid or plastic wrap.
5. Drain the cashews and blend them with ½ cup of fresh water until creamy. Add the contents of the saucepan, as much of the roasted garlic as you like (i like the whole head), lemon juice and salt to taste and blend until creamy. Add as much of the remaining ½ cup of vegetable stock as you want to reach the consistency that you like.
6. Serve the soup hot or chill it in the fridge for a couple of hours and serve cold. Garnish with pomegranate seeds and herbs, if desired.

Nutrition Value
Calories: 219kcal Carbohydrates: 34g Protein: 6g Fat: 7g Saturated Fat: 1g Sodium: 671mg Potassium: 597mg Fiber: 5g Sugar: 10g

83. Green Pizza With Herbed Vegan Cashew Cheese

Cook Time: 20 Minutes
Total Time: 20 Minutes

Ingredients
- 3/4 cup (115 grams) raw cashews soaked overnight or in hot water for 10 minutes
- 1 clove of garlic roughly chopped
- 1 ¼ packed cups (65 grams) cilantro leaves and stems
- ½ packed cup (13 grams) mint leaves only
- 1 teaspoon sea salt
- Juice of 1 lime
- 1 ½ tablespoons nutritional yeast optional
- 3/4 cup (175 ml) water
- 1 pizza crust store-bought or homemade
- 6 asparagus cut into bite-sized pieces
- ¼ cup (60 ml) balsamic vinegar
- 1/2 a small red onion
- A small bag of mixed baby greens
- 1/2 an avocado diced

Instructions
1. Combine all the ingredients from the cashews to the water in a blender or food processor and blitz into a paste.
2. Bake the pizza crust according to the package (or your recipe) directions half-way through until the crust is just beginning to turn brown. Take it out of the oven and spread the cashew cheese on top. You may not have to use all the cashew cheese now, reserve any leftovers to dollop on top of the baked crust. Continue baking the crust until is golden brown.
3. Meanwhile, make the balsamic reduction by heating the vinegar in a small pot over medium-low heat. Reduce until the vinegar can coat the back of a spoon and is reduced by about half.
4. Heat a small pan over medium heat and add a couple tablespoons of water and the asparagus. Cover and cook until tender, then remove the asparagus from the pan and reserve.
5. When the crust is baked, dollop over any remaining cashew cheese, sprinkle with red onion and top with the greens, diced avocado and asparagus. Drizzle over the balsamic reduction and serve.

Nutrition Facts
Calories: 488kcal Carbohydrates: 65g Protein: 16g Fat: 19g Saturated Fat: 4g Sodium: 1127mg Potassium: 522mg Fiber: 5g Sugar: 6g

84. Green Goddess Vegan Broccoli Soup

Prep Time: 10 Minutes
Cook Time: 15 Minutes
Total Time: 25 Minutes

Ingredients
- 2 tbsp coconut oil
- 1 small yellow onion diced
- 1 leek cleaned and sliced
- 2 cloves garlic minced
- 1 head broccoli
- 2 cups vegetable broth
- 1 head of kale chopped and divided
- 3 tbsp flour
- 2 cups non dairy milk i used almond milk but coconut milk works too
- 1 tsp salt
- 1/2 tsp pepper
- 1/2 tsp red pepper flakes
- Pumpkin seeds for garnish
- Kale chips
- 2 cups kale chopped
- 1 tbsp olive oil
- Salt & pepper to taste

Instructions
1. Preheat oven to 400 f. Wash and chop kale, then dry thoroughly before tossing 2 cups of it with 1 tbsp olive oil, massaging oil into leaves and seasoning with salt before spreading onto a parchment-lined baking sheet.
2. Set aside for now.
3. Melt coconut oil in a large pot on med-high heat. Saute onions, leek and garlic.
4. Whisk in flour, then gradually add your non-dairy milk, salt and pepper, whisking until thickened.
5. Stir in vegetable broth, then add broccoli, bringing to a boil then simmering for 5 min until broccoli is tender.
6. Remove from heat, and stir in 2 cups of chopped kale, letting cool for about 15 min before pureeing vegetables in a blender
7. While waiting for the soup to cool, you can make your kale chips!
8. Bake them in the preheated oven for 7-8 min, checking and flipping them every couple minutes so they don't burn. When they're crispy, remove them from the oven and set aside to top your soup with.
9. Puree your soup in a blender, then serve with pumpkin seeds and kale chips garnished on top. Enjoy!

Nutrition Facts
Calories: 159kcal Carbohydrates: 18g Protein: 6g Fat: 9g Saturated Fat: 4g Sodium: 862mg Potassium: 544mg Fiber: 4g Sugar: 4g Vitamin A: 4276iu Vitamin C: 132mg Calcium: 212mg Iron: 2mg

85. Lean Green Burger

Total Time: 15

Ingredients
- 1 morningstar farms grillers original
- 1/4 small zucchini
- 2 tablespoons finely chopped cucumber
- 1 tablespoon low-fat plain yogurt
- 1/2 teaspoon chopped fresh dill or 1/4 teaspoon dried dillweed
- 1/8 teaspoon lemon-pepper seasoning salt
- 2 lettuce leaves
- 2 very thin tomato slices
- 2 teaspoons chopped red onion

Instructions

1. Cook morningstar farms grillers original veggie burger according to package directions.
2. Meanwhile, use vegetable peeler to lengthwise cut zucchini into very thin strips. Set aside. In small bowl stir together cucumber, yogurt, dill and seasoning salt.
3. Serve burger in lettuce leaves with tomato, zucchini, yogurt mixture and red onion.

Nutritional Value
Fat: 6g Sat Fat: 1g Sodium: 290mg Potassium: 380mg Carbohydrate: 9g Fiber: 3g Sugar: 4g Protein: 17g

86. Lean Green Lettuce Tacos

Prep Time: 15 Mins
Cook Time: 11 Mins
Total Time: 26 Mins

Ingredients
- 1 small zucchini, diced
- 1 small yellow squash, diced
- ½ pound extra-lean ground beef
- 1 tablespoon olive oil
- 1 (1.25-oz.) Taco fresco seasoning
- 1 (8-oz.) Can no-salt-added tomato sauce
- 2 tablespoons chopped fresh cilantro
- 1 tablespoon lime juice
- 8 romaine lettuce leaves

Instructions
1. Sauté first 3 ingredients in hot oil in a large nonstick skillet over medium-high heat for 5 to 6 minutes or until meat crumbles and is no longer pink. Stir in seasoning until blended; cook 1 minute.
2. Reduce heat to low; stir in tomato sauce, and cook, stirring often, 3 to 4 minutes or until thoroughly heated. Remove from heat, and stir in cilantro and lime juice.
3. Serve meat mixture in romaine lettuce leaves with desired toppings.
4. 2% reduced-fat shredded cheddar or monterey jack cheese may be substituted.

Nutrition Facts
Fat: 4.5g Saturated Fat: 1.3g Protein: 6.7g Carbohydrates : 6.2g Fiber: 1g Cholesterol: 10mg Iron: 1mg Sodium: 227mg Calcium: 14mg.

87. Spicy Steamed Greens With Hemp Seeds

Prep Time: 10 Minutes
Cook Time: 5 Minutes
Total Time: 15 Minutes

Ingredients
- 1 large bunch of asparagus, ends removed and chopped in half
- 1 broccoli, cut up into segments
- 1 large zucchini, sliced into thick strips
- 1 tbsp of tamari
- 2 garlic cloves
- ¼ cup of hemp seeds
- 1 fresh chili, chopped (optional)
- Salt and black pepper to taste

Instructions
1. Steam the greens for 5 minutes, or until cooked to your liking. (try not to overcook.)
2. Place the vegetables on a platter and sprinkle the remaining ingredients over the greens.
3. Serve immediately and enjoy!

Nutritional Value
Carbohydrates: 61g Protein: 11g Fat: 2g Saturated Fat: 0g Cholesterol: 0mg Sodium: 410mg Potassium: 2224mg Fiber: 11g Sugar: 10g

88. Summer Zoodle Primavera

Prep Time: 10 Minutes
Cook Time: 20 Minutes
Total Time: 30 Minutes

Ingredients
Pasta Ingredients:
- 1 large zucchini
- 1 large orange bell pepper (capsicum)
- 1 cup cherry tomatoes
- 6 large leaves of kale
- 1 tbsp fresh oregano
- 1 tbsp fresh basil

Sauce Ingredients:
- 32 oz pomi strained tomatoes (or cook down about 12 large fresh tomatoes) see this fresh, easy herb tomato sauce recipe for more sauce ideas using fresh tomatoes.
- 3 garlic cloves
- 4 tbsp fresh oregano
- 4 tbsp fresh basil
- 2 tsp cumin
- 1 tsp honey
- 1 tbsp extra virgin olive oil
- Sea salt/himalayan salt and fresh ground black pepper, to taste

Instructions
Pasta Instructions:
1. Wash all produce well.
2. Insert zucchini into spiralizer and twist over a bowl to create noodles.
3. Chop pepper, tomatoes, and kale.
4. Add chopped veggies to bowl with zoodles.
5. Chop oregano and basil then add to bowl.
6. Serve into bowls then top with sauce.

Sauce Instructions:
8. Place pot on the stove top over medium-low heat.
9. Add olive oil.
10. Smash garlic to remove peel then chop.
11. Add garlic to olive oil after it's slightly warm.
12. Let cook for about 2 minutes, then pour in strained tomatoes.
13. Chop herbs then add to the sauce.
14. Add cumin, honey, salt, and pepper.
15. Reduce heat to low and let cook for about 15-20 minutes, stirring occasionally, tasting and adjusting spices as desired.
16. Pour sauce over zoodles, then top with more fresh herbs and enjoy!

Nutritional Value
Calories: 170 Fat: 1g Sodium: 610mg Carbohydrates: 28g Fiber: 8g Sugars: 8g Protein: 7g

89. Lean Green Bean Salad

Prep Time: 10 Mins
Cook Time: 3 Mins
Total Time: 13 Mins

Ingredients
- 100g green beans (21 calories)

- 75g (1/2 cup) zucchini, halved lengthways, and sliced
- 50g baby spinach
- 100g asparagus, cut into diagonal lengths
- 125g cherry tomatoes, halved
- 4 olives, sliced

Dressing:
- 2 tsp olive oil
- ½ tbs balsamic vinegar

Instructions
1. Steam beans, asparagus, and zucchini until just cooked and still a little crisp. Refresh under cold water. Add into a large bowl with spinach, tomatoes, and olives. Refrigerate until ready to serve.
2. Drizzle salad with combined oil and vinegar and serve immediately.
3. Eat mindfully and enjoy

Nutrition Information
Sat fat: 1.5g Carbohydrates: 7.8g Fiber: 3.7g Sugar: 1.5g Protein: 4g Calcium: 81mg Iron: 1mg Potassium: 230mg Sodium: 215mmg

90. Green Salad With Beets, Oranges & Avocado

Prep time: 10 minutes
Total time: 10 minutes

Ingredients
- 4 cups leafy greens (i used a chard/kale/arugula/spinach mix)
- 3 small oranges, peeled and sliced into rounds
- 1 avocado, peeled, pitted, and diced
- 1 large carrot, peeled and julienned
- 1 small beet, peeled and julienned
- 1/2 cup crumbled feta or goat cheese
- 1/4 cup toasted pepitas
- 1/3 cup white balsamic vinaigrette (or any vinaigrette)

Instructions
1. Add greens, oranges, avocado, carrot, beets, pepitas, and cheese together in a large bowl.
2. Drizzle evenly with the vinaigrette, and toss until the salad is combined and evenly coated.
3. Serve immediately, topped with some freshly-cracked black pepper if desired.

Nutritional facts
Carbohydrates: 10g Protein: 15g Fat: 8g Saturatedfat: 1g Cholesterol: 61mg Sodium: 349mg Potassium: 589mg Fiber: 3g Sugar: 5g Calcium: 36mg Iron: 0.7mg

91. Avocado Cream Of Mushroom Soup

Prep Time: 10 Minutes
Cook Time: 15 Minutes
Total Time: 25 Minutes

Ingredients
- 2 avocados, peeled and pitted
- Juice of 1 lemon
- 1 clove garlic
- 2 cups hot water
- 1 tbsp (15 ml) coconut oil
- 1 cup (128 g) mushrooms, sliced
- 1 red pepper (capsicum), diced
- 1/4 small yellow onion, finely minced
- 2 tomatoes, diced
- 3-4 sprigs of fresh basil

Instructions
1. In a food processor or high-powered blender, blend avocado, lemon juice, garlic, and hot water. Set aside.

2. Heat coconut oil in a medium pan with tall sides over medium-high heat.
3. Sauté mushrooms, red pepper (capsicum), onion, tomato, and basil until they begin to soften.
4. Add avocado mixture and heat through.

Nutritional Facts
Calories: 230 Fat: 18g Trans fat: 5g Cholesterol: 0mg Sodium: 20mg Carbohydrates: 17g Fiber: 8g Sugars: 6g Protein: 4g

92. Raw Curry Cauliflower Soup

Prep Time: 15 Minutes
Cook Time: 5 Minutes
Total Time: 20 Minutes

Ingredients
- 1/3 cup raw cashews
- 1 cup (250 ml) fresh young thai coconut water & coconut
- 2 tsp extra virgin olive oil
- 1 medium shallot
- 1 medium head cauliflower, cut into 1-inch pieces
- 2 tbsp curry powder (i use vindaloo curry powder for more heat)
- 1 tsp ground turmeric
- 1 tsp ground cumin
- 5 drops stevia (optional and to taste)
- 1/4 tsp ground cinnamon
- Himalayan salt, to taste
- 1/4 cup chopped fresh cilantro

Garnish:
- Cubed avocado
- Apple chopped into sticks
- Trail mix /pepitas, coconut raisins, assorted nuts & sunflower seeds for crunch

Instructions
1. Blend all ingredients except garnish in a high-speed blender until slightly warm, about 4 – 5 minutes.
2. Garnish with preferred toppings and enjoy!

Nutritional Value
Calories: 130g Fat: 6g Trans fat: 0g Cholesterol: 0mg Sodium: 110mg Carbohydrates: 15g Fiber: 5g Sugars: 7g Protein: 5g

93. Chlorophyll-Rich Green Soup

Prep Time: 15 Minutes
Cook Time: 15 Minutes
Total Time: 30 Minutes

Ingredients
- 1 tbsp olive oil or coconut oil
- 1 leek, sliced
- 3 cloves of garlic, crushed
- 1/2 head of broccoli, chopped
- 4 kale leaves, chopped
- 1 zucchini, chopped
- 500 g of baby peas (fresh or frozen)
- 3 cups (750 ml) vegetable broth or vegetable stock
- 1 small handful of fresh parsley or 1 tsp dried
- Salt and pepper, to taste
- 1 tsp dried oregano
- 1 tsp dried tarragon

Instructions
1. Wash, prepare, chop and slice vegetables.
2. Heat oil in medium size pot and sauté over a low to medium heat the leeks and garlic until translucent.
3. Add in the broccoli, kale, and zucchini and stir for a few minutes.

4. Add the peas and stock and bring to the boil then turn down the heat.
5. Add remaining ingredients and simmer for 10 minutes or until the vegetables are soft.
6. Once cooked, use a stick blender and blend the soup to form a smoother texture or leave a little chunky. You can also use a normal blender or chop vegetables into bite size pieces and leave super chunky.
7. Add in any fresh herbs for garnish (optional) and serve immediately.

Nutritional Value
Sodium: 190mg Carbohydrates: 21g Fiber: 6g Sugars: 2g Protein: 6g

SEAFOOD RECIPES

94. Smoky Shrimp Chipotle

Prep Time: 5 Minutes
Cook Time: 15 Minutes
Total Time: 20 Minutes
Servings: 4 Serving

Ingredients
- 4 teaspoons of oil of your choice and fresh garlic
- 1 C chopped chives or scallions (greens only)
- 2 lbs wild-caught, raw shrimp, shelled, deveined & tails removed
- 1 can (~16 oz) diced tomatoes (unflavored, no sugar added)
- 1 capful (1 Tablespoon)
- 4 lime wedges (optional)
- 4 T fresh cilantro (optional)

Instructions

1. Heat oil in a medium-sized frying pan over medium-high heat.
2. Add the scallions and cook for one minute, until slightly wilted and glistening.
3. Add the shrimp and cook for 1 minute on each side.
4. Add the tomatoes and Cinnamon Chipotle seasoning. Cook an additional 3-5 minutes, stirring occasionally until the tomatoes are hot and shrimp is opaque & fully cooked. Be careful not to overcook as it will make the shrimp tough and dry.
5. Sprinkle with cilantro if desired and spritz with a wedge of lime (or serve the lime wedge on the plate for a pretty and functional garnish.
6. Serve warm.
7. Makes about 4 servings.

Nutrition
Calories: 250 Total Fat: 3.6g Sat Fat: 1.1g Cholesterol: 418mg Sodium: 487mgCarbohydrates: 6.2g Fiber: 1.5g Sugar: 1.4g Protein: 46.1g Calcium: 207gIron: 1mg Potassium: 485mg

95. Seared Scallops in Creamy Garlic Sauce

Cook Time: 15 Minutes
Total Time: 20 Minutes
Servings: 4 Serving

Ingredients
- Nonstick cooking spray
- 2 lbs dry sea scallops
- 1 tsp of salt pepper garlic onion and parsley)
- 3/4 C chicken stock, vegetable stock, fish stock, or dry white wine
- 2 T butter
- 3/4 C Half and Half

Instructions
1. Spray a large nonstick pan with nonstick cooking spray and place on the stove over high heat.
2. When the pan is hot, add scallops, leaving space in between them, don't crowd or they will not cook evenly. Sprinkle with a little light dusting of Dash of Desperation.
3. Cook on high heat for about 7-8 minutes, until they have a lovely brown coating on them.
4. Flip each scallop over using tongs and cook an additional minute or two on the opposite side. Scallops will be done when they turn opaque. Remove the scallops from the pan and place them in a dish to the side. Return the pan to the stove.
5. Stir in the butter until melted to make a quick pan sauce. Be sure to scrape any "bits" from the bottom of the pan for additional flavor.
6. Add the stock, half and half, and Garlic Seasoning. Heat on high until boiling then reduce heat to medium-high and let simmer until liquid is reduced by half.
7. Add scallops back to the pan and toss to coat with the sauce and reheat. Divide into four equal portions and serve immediately with your favorite side dish.

Nutrition
Calories: 320 Total Fat: 5.3g Sat Fat: 1.3g Cholesterol: 143mg Sodium: 137mg Carbohydrates: 7.3g Fiber: 3.7g Sugar: 4g Protein: 68g Calcium: 21mg Iron: 3mg Potassium: 1118mg

96.	Tender And Tasty Fish Tacos

Prep Time: 15 Minutes
Cook Time: 15 Minutes
Total Time: 30 Minutes
Servings: 4 Serving

Ingredients
- 1 3/4 lbs cod or haddock (wild-caught)
- 1 capful (1 tablespoon)
- Phoenix sunrise seasoning or cumin, cilantro, garlic, onion, red pepper, paprika, parsley, salt & pepper (or low sodium taco seasoning)
- 4 teaspoons of oil of your choice and fresh garlic
- Your favorite taco condiments (for a list of quantities and Lean & Green approved condiments.

Instructions
1. Pat fish dry and cut into 1" chunks
2. Sprinkle seasoning over fish and toss to coat.
3. Heat Roasted Garlic Oil in a large, nonstick frying pan over medium-high heat.
4. Add fish and cook for 10 - 12 minutes, until fish is opaque and breaks apart into flakes. Be careful not to overcook or the fish will be dry and chewy.
5. Serve hot with your favorite condiments.
6. Makes about 4 servings.

Nutrition
Calories: 151 Total Fat: 1.3g Sat Fat: 0.3g Cholesterol: 78mg Sodium: 111mg Carbohydrates: 0.2g Fiber: 0.1g Sugar: 0g Protein: 32.5g Calcium: 25mg Iron: 1mg Potassium: 355mg

97.	Summer Shrimp Primavera

Prep Time: 10 Minutes
Cook Time: 10-15 Minutes
Total Time: 20-25 Minutes
Servings: 4 Servings

Ingredients
- 4 teaspoons Luscious Lemon or Roasted Garlic Oil

- 2 pounds wild-caught shrimp, raw, peeled & deveined
- 1 Tablespoon of sea salt, scallions, fresh garlic, lemon & parsley)
- 1/2 C low sodium chicken broth
- 6 C vegetable noodles
- 1 scallion, green tops only, sliced for garnish if desired
- 8 T fresh grated Parmesan cheese for garnish

Instructions

1. Make the vegetable noodles by spiralizing or using a vegetable peeler like I did to make big, wide noodles. Place noodles in a bowl and set aside.
2. Place the oil in the pan over medium-high heat and let it get hot.
3. Add the shrimp to the pan and cook for 3-4 minutes on one side before turning to cook on the other side. Sprinkle with seasoning and continue to cook for an additional 3 minutes. Add the broth to deglaze the pan and cook 1-2 minutes more, until shrimp are fully cooked.
4. Using a slotted spoon, remove the shrimp from the pan and set it aside in a bowl.
5. Put the pan back over heat and heat until the liquid is bubbling. Add the veggie noodles and saute for 1-2 minutes, until crisp-tender.
6. Add the veggie noodles to a serving bowl. Top with the shrimp and sprinkle with scallions and Parmesan cheese before serving.
7. Divide everything into 4 equal portions and serve hot.

Nutrition

Calories: 281 Total Fat: 9g Sat Fat: 2.4g Cholesterol: 392mg Sodium: 535mg Carbohydrates: 3.4g Fiber: 0.2g Sugar: .1g Protein: 44g Calcium: 234mg Iron: 1mg Potassium: 334mg

98. Garlic Shrimp & Broccoli

Prep Time: 15 Minutes
Cook Time: 10 Minutes
Total Time: 25 Minutes
Servings: 4 Serving

Ingredients

- 4 teaspoons Roasted Garlic Oil (or fresh garlic and oil of your choice)
- 1 3/4 lbs wild-caught shrimp, thawed and shells removed
- 2 C fresh broccoli florets
- 2 teaspoon Rockin' Ranch Seasoning (or tarragon, black pepper, salt, lemon, parsley, chives, garlic, and onion)
- 1 teaspoon Garlic Gusto, Garlic & Spring Onion or Simply Brilliant Seasoning (or fresh garlic, lemon, and onion)
- 1/3 C low sodium chicken broth
- 4 C alternative "noodles" of your choice
- 2 Tablespoons butter

Instructions

1. Add oil to a large frying pan (with a lid) over medium-high heat.
2. When the oil is hot, add shrimp and cook for 1 minute on each side until slightly pink.
3. Add seasonings and broth to the shrimp. Stir to combine.
4. Add broccoli and place the cover on the pan. Bring to a boil and reduce heat to medium. Cook until broccoli is bright green (about 2 minutes).
5. Remove the cover and add the butter. Stir to combine and then add the noodles. Toss the noodles in the liquid and cook until hot. Serve immediately.

Nutrition
Calories: 340 Total Fat: 12g Sat Fat: 4g Cholesterol: 398mg Sodium: 511mg Carbohydrates: 12.4g Fiber: 3.3g Sugar: 4.2g Protein: 41g Calcium: 219mg Iron: 2mg Potassium: 971mg

99. Spinach Pesto With Couscous And Shrimp

Prep Time: 5 Mins
Cook Time: 15 Mins
Total Time: 20 Mins

Ingredients
- 5 oz 142 grams spinach (one clamshell of baby spinach)
- 1 cup fresh basil leaves
- 1/4 cup pine nuts
- 1 clove garlic
- 1/4 cup olive oil
- 1/2 medium lemon, grind and pith (white layer underneath skin) removed
- 1/4 tsp sea salt
- 2 cups israeli couscous (pearl couscous)
- 4 cups cold water
- 400 grams raw prawns or shrimp
- 1 tbsp olive oil
- 1/4 tsp crushed red pepper flakes

Instructions
1. Bring 4 cups of salted water to a boil. Add couscous, cover, and reduce heat. Cook, undisturbed for 15 minutes. Fluff with a fork.
2. Meanwhile, place spinach, basil, pin nuts, garlic clove, 1/4 cup olive oil, 1/2 lemon (with grind and pith removed), and 1/4 tsp sea salt into a blender. Blend until smooth. Pour over cooked couscous and mix until fully coated.
3. In a medium bowl, toss together prawns, olive oil, and red pepper flakes. Heat a large skillet to medium-high and cooked prawns until pink, turning once. About 6-7 minutes total.
4. Top pesto couscous with prawns and serve.

100. Pea & Mint Soup With Thai Shrimp Skewers

Prep Time: 10 Mins
Cook Time: 15 Mins
Total Time: 25 Mins

Ingredients
- For the pea & mint soup
- 1 bunch spring onions trimmed and roughly chopped
- 1 medium potato peeled and diced
- 1 garlic clove minced
- 850 ml vegetable stock
- 250 g/9oz shelled young peas
- 4 tbsp chopped fresh mint
- 1 tbsp fresh thyme leaves
- Large pinch caster sugar
- 1 tbsp fresh lemon or lime juice

For The Thai Shrimp Skewers:
- 16 fresh shrimps / king prawns cleaned
- Zest of 1 lime
- 2 tbsp olive oil
- ½ tsp of sesame oil
- Finely chopped thai chili to taste

Instructions
1. Set 2 tbsp of chopped spring onion aside. Put the remaining ones into a large pan with the potato, garlic, thyme and stock.
2. Bring to the boil, lower the heat and simmer for 15 mins.
3. Add peas to the soup and simmer for 3 minutes. Season to taste.
4. Save 2 tbsp of cooked peas in a container to garnish the dish.
5. Stir into the soup mint, sugar and lemon or lime juice, then pour into a food processor and blend until smooth.
6. Garnish with the reserved peas, chopped onion, thyme leaves and salt and pepper to taste.

For The Thai Shrimp Skewers:
1. Mix together olive & sesame oil, lime zest, chili, salt and pepper to taste.
2. Thread 4 shrimps through each skewer at two points, through the neck and tail portion.
3. Brush the oil mix on both sides of each skewer, and sprinkle with sesame seeds.
4. Heat until hot a medium grilling pan. Place the skewers and grill for 2 mins on each side, until cooked through.

101. Skewered Shrimp With Leeks And Yellow Squash

Prep Time: 15 Minutes
Cook Time: 15-20 Minutes
Total Time: 25-30 Minutes
Servings: 4 Servings

Ingredients
- 2 pounds wild-caught shrimp, raw, peeled & deveined
- 2 large leeks, washed, trimmed, and cut into 1/2" chunks
- 2 small, thinner yellow squash, washed, trimmed, and cut into 1/2" chunks
- 1 Tablespoon of tarragon, chives, garlic, lemon, salt, pepper, garlic, and onion)
- 2 1/2 Tablespoons Stacey Hawkins Luscious Lemon or Roasted Garlic Oil
- 8 T fresh grated Parmesan cheese for garnish
- Natural Sea salt & freshly cracked peppercorns (or a pinch of Dash of Desperation) to taste

Instructions
1. Preheat outdoor grill or oven to 375 degrees.
2. Add the shrimp and veggies to a large bowl. Drizzle with oil and seasonings. Toss to coat. Let sit for 10 minutes, up to all day (refrigerated) to let the flavors develop.
3. Skewer shrimp and veggies individually, or pour into a grill basket.
4. Cook for 20-25 minutes, using a spatula to turn the pieces at least once during cooking. Cook until shrimp is opaque and fully cooked and vegetables are crisp-tender.
5. Serve hot, sprinkled with fresh grated Parmesan cheese for a garnish,

Nutrition
Calories: 352 Total Fat: 13.3g Sat Fat: 3g Cholesterol: 455mg Sodium: 784mg Carbohydrates: 12.3g Fiber: 2.4g Sugar: 4.4g Protein: 47.9g Calcium: 53mg Iron: 2mg Potassium: 449mg

102. Thai Sweet Chili Salmon Soba Noodles

Prep Time: 10 Mins

Cook Time: 10 Mins
Total Time: 20 Mins

Ingredients
- 200 gr fresh skin-on salmon fillet
- 2 tbsp thai sweet chili sauce
- 1 tbsp fresh lime juice
- Shichimi to taste (optional)
- 150 gr broccolini
- 1 medium carrot peeled and julienned (cut into fine matchsticks)
- 80 gr frozen peas defrosted
- 150 gr soba noodles i used gluten-free black soba noodles
- 2 spring onions finely sliced
- A handful of cilantro finely chopped
- 2 tbsp black sesame seeds optional
- Good-quality olive oil
- Sea salt

Instructions
1. In a small bowl, mix together sweet chili sauce, lime juice and shichimi (if using). Add the salmon, coat well with the mixture and leave to marinate for 10 min.
2. Heat a large skillet with a glug of olive oil over medium heat. Lift the salmon from the marinade, season with salt and cook skin down for 2 min, then turn on the other side and cook a further 2 min.
3. Take the salmon off the pan, remove the skin, and chop into bite-sized chunks (it should still be raw in the center).
4. Heat the skillet again with another swirl of olive oil, then fold in peas, carrot sticks and broccolini and stir-fry for 2 min. Pour in the salmon and its marinade, add a bit of water, and cook for 2 min, then remove from the heat.
5. In the meantime, cook the noodles following pack instructions. Drain well, and fold them into the pan with the other ingredients. Toss in spring onion, sesame seeds (optional) and cilantro, and mix everything together.
6. For a bit of extra kick, mix in another glug of sweet chili sauce and serve immediately.

103. Easy Healthy Cucumber Tomato Avocado Salad Recipe

Prep Time: 15 Minutes
Total Time: 15 Minutes

Ingredients
- 2 tbsp lemon juice
- 2 tbsp olive oil
- 1/2 tsp garlic powder
- 1/2 tsp sea salt (to taste)
- 1/4 tsp black pepper (to taste)
- 2 large hass avocados (halved, pitted, peeled, and cubed)*
- 6 medium tomato (cut into wedges)
- 2 cups english cucumber (chopped)
- 3 tbsp fresh dill (chopped)
- 3 tbsp fresh parsley (chopped)

Instructions
1. **For The Dressing:** in a small bowl, whisk together the lemon juice, olive oil, garlic powder, sea salt, and black pepper. (alternatively, place in an airtight container and shake vigorously.)
5. In a large bowl, combine the avocado, tomatoes, cucumber, fresh dill, and fresh parsley.
6. Pour the dressing over the salad and toss to coat. Serve immediately.

Nutrition Information
Calories: 150 Fat: 12g Protein: 2g Total carbs: 10g Net carbs: 5g Fiber: 5g Sugar: 4g

104. Vegan Scallops With Spring Greens

Prep Time: 10 Mins
Cook Time: 6 Mins
Total Time: 16 Mins

Ingredients
- 2 king oyster mushroom tops removed
- 1 cup fresh/frozen baby peas
- 4 asparagus blanched and chopped into chunks
- A bunch of baby green leaves to serve
- 2 thyme sprigs
- 1 garlic clove lightly mashed
- 4-5 fresh mint leaves
- Extravirgin olive oil
- Salt and pepper freshly cracked

Instructions
1. Cut the mushroom stems into scallops-like, around 2inch each.
2. Soak them into a container filled with warm water for at least 1h or overnight.
3. Boil the peas for 3-4 minutes, drain and cool under cold running water.
4. Fold the peas into a blender with mint, and salt and pepper to taste. Drizzle with oil and blend until smooth and creamy. Reserve until ready to serve.
5. Pat the mushroom scallops dry. Drizzle a pan with olive oil, ad thyme and garlic and heat over med-high heat.
6. Add vegan scallops and grill 3-4 mins on each side, or until crisp and lightly brown and cooked through.
7. Arrange a bunch of baby leaves on a plate, spoon the pea puree over, add chopped asparagus and scallops.
8. Season with freshly cracked pepper and sea salt flakes and serve immediately.

105. Mediterranean Chopped Salad With Shrimp

Prep Time: 15 Mins
Total: 15 Mins

Ingredients
- ½ head romaine lettuce, cut crosswise into thin strips (8 cups)
- 1 pound cooked peeled and deveined medium shrimp, cut in half crosswise
- ½ english cucumber, chopped
- 1 15.5-ounce can chickpeas, rinsed; or a heaping 1/2 cup dried chickpeas, soaked and cooked
- ½ medium sweet onion (such as vidalia or walla walla), chopped
- ¾ cup crumbled feta (about 3 ounces)
- ½ cup pitted kalamata olives, halved
- 2 cups pita chips, broken into pieces
- 3 tablespoons olive oil
- 2 tablespoons red wine vinegar
- Kosher salt and black pepper

Instructions
1. In a large bowl, toss the lettuce, shrimp, cucumber, chickpeas, onion, feta, olives, and pita chips with the oil, vinegar, and ¼ teaspoon each salt and pepper.

Nutrition Facts
Fat: 24g Saturated Fat: 6g Cholesterol: 191mg Sodium: 1065mg Protein: 33g Carbohydrates: 31g Sugars: 6g Fiber: 6g; Iron: 5mg Calcium: 264mg.

106. Lemony Spinach & Salmon Fusilli

Prep Time: 5 Mins
Cook Time: 10 Mins
Total Time: 15 Mins

Ingredients
- 160 gr short pasta (fusilli, penne, rigatoni)
- 150 gr fresh cleaned salmon fillet cut into cubes
- 175 g cherry tomatoes halved
- Salt & black pepper
- 5-6 fresh basil leaves
- 225 gr fresh spinach leaves
- 1 shallot finely minced
- 1 tbsp extra virgin olive oil
- A pinch of brown sugar
- 1 tsp lemon zest

Instructions
1. Heat a large pot of lightly salted water to a boil. Toss in the pasta and cook until al dente, about 9 min.
2. In the meantime, heat the olive oil in a large skillet over med-low heat. Add in the shallots and sautee' until soft.
3. Fold the tomatoes in, season with salt, pepper and a pinch of sugar. Cook for about 5 mins, stirring every now and then.
4. Add chopped salmon into the pan and stir-fry for 2 mins. Add in basil and spinach leaves and cook for 4 more mins, or until the greens soften and the salmon is cooked through.
5. Drain pasta and toss into the pan with the other ingredients.
6. Add freshly grated lemon zest. Mix all ingredients together and remove from the heat.
7. Season with extra freshly cracked black pepper and serve immediately.

SMOOTHIES

107. Lean & Green Smoothie

Active: 5 mins
Total: 10 mins
Servings: 4

Ingredients
- 2 ½ cups stemmed kale leaves
- 1 cup cubed pineapple
- ¾ cup apple juice, chilled
- ½ cup seedless green grapes, frozen
- ½ cup chopped Granny Smith apple
- 1 cup Halved green grapes

Instructions
1. Place kale, pineapple, apple juice, frozen grapes, and apple in a blender.
2. Cover and blend until smooth, about 3 minutes.
3. If desired, garnish smoothies with halved grapes.

Nutrition
Per Serving: 81 calories; protein 2g; carbohydrates 19g; dietary fiber 2g; sugars 14g; fat 1g; sodium 19mg.

108. 41. Superfood Green Smoothie

Prep Time: 5 Mins
Total Time: 5 Mins

Ingredients
- ½ avocado, peeled & pitted
- 1 banana
- ½ cup spinach
- ½ cup ice cubes
- 1 cup almond milk
- 1 tbsp vegan protein powder, clink link for the one i recommend
- 1 tbsp flaxseed
- 1 tsp honey
- ¼ tsp ground cinnamon

Instructions
1. Add the avocado, banana, spinach, ice cubes, and almond milk to a blender.
2. Add the protein powder, flaxseed, honey, and ground cinnamon.
3. Blend until smooth and creamy.

Nutrition Facts
Carbohydrates 46g Protein 12g Fat 23g Saturated Fat 3g Sodium 419mg Potassium 1075mg Fiber 14g Sugar 21g

109. Tasty Lean Green Smoothie

Prep: 5 Min

Ingredients
- 3/4 cup coconut water
- 1/2 tbsp chia seeds
- 1/2 cup baby spinach leaves
- 1/4 avocado
- 1/4 bunch mint, leaves picked, reserving some leaves to garnish
- 1 tsp almond butter
- 1/2 medium banana
- 30g vanilla protein powder
- 1/2 cup ice cubes

Instructions
1. Add coconut water and chia seeds to the blender and stand for 2 minutes.
2. Add remaining ingredients to the blender and blitz until smooth. Pour into a glass and garnish with chia seeds and a few mint leaves.

Nutritional Information
Energy: 1415.98 Kj Calories: 338.23 Cals Protein: 26.60g Fibre: 7.71g Fat: 13.32g Sat. Fat: 2.52g Carbs: 24.82g Sugar: 20.22g

110. Slim Down Greens Smoothie

Total Time: 10 Mins
Ingredients
- 1 scoop gnc earth genius core slimming greens
- 1 cup vanilla, unsweetened almond milk
- 1 cup fresh baby spinach
- ½ fresh, medium-sized apple
- 1 scoop gnc earth genius soy protein (unflavored)
- 1 tbsp. Dried chia seeds
- 1 cup ice

Instructions
1. Add all ingredients to a high-powered food processor and blend until smooth.
2. Add additional ice as needed to reach desired consistency.

Nutritional Value
Calories: 250   Fat: 7g;   Sodium: 450mg   Fiber: 11g
Carbohydrates: 31g   Sugars: 12g   Protein: 18g

111. Green Keto Smoothie

Prep Time: 1 Minute
Ingredients
- 1/2 avocado
- 1/3 cucumber
- 2 cups spinach
- 6 oz coconut milk
- 6 oz almond milk (unsweetened)
- 1 tsp matcha powder
- 1/2 lime juice only
- 1/2 scoop low sugar vanilla protein powder
- 1/2 tsp chia seeds to garnish

Instructions
1. Place spinach and coconut milk in a blender, blitz to break down spinach to make room for other
2. Add all other ingredients and blend until smooth

Nutrition Facts
Protein: 2g   Carbohydrates: 19g   Dietary Fiber: 2g
Sugars: 14g   Fat: 1g   Sodium: 19mg.

112. Non-Dairy Lean Mean Fighting Machine Smoothie Recipe

Prep Time: 5 Minutes
Ingredients
- 1 cup almond milk unsweetened
- 1 1/2 cup strawberries
- 2 cups spinach
- 1 frozen banana
- 1 tbsp raw walnuts
- 1 tbsp flax seeds
- 1 tbsp chia seeds
- 1/2 tsp cinnamon
- 1 inch fresh ginger
- Zest of 1/2 lemon
- Juice of 1/2 lemon
- Pinch sea salt
- 1 cup ice

Instructions
1. Place all ingredients as listed in a vitamix or other high-powered blender.
2. If using the vitamix, choose the 'frozen desserts' setting.
3. For a thinner consistency, add more water and for more froth, add more ice. Enjoy!

Nutrition Facts
Protein: 2g Carbohydrates: 19g Dietary Fiber: 2g Sugars: 14g Fat: 1g Sodium: 19mg

113. 46. Green Apple Smoothie

Total Time: 10 Mins
Ingredients
- 1 serving vanilla
- 1 big handful of your favorite mild-tasting greens, such as spinach, chard, baby kale, or romaine lettuce
- 1 cup unsweetened almond milk
- 1 granny smith apple, cored
- 1/4 ripe avocado, pitted and skin removed
- 1 lime, skin completely removed, flesh only
- 1/2 tsp vanilla extract
- 6 ice cubes

Instructions
1. Add all ingredients except ice to the (or your blender of choice) and blend until smooth.
2. Toss in the ice cubes and continue blending until no chunks remain.
3. Pour into a glass and enjoy.

Nutritional Value
Protein:1.6g Carbohydrates: 21.2g Fat: 0.5g Sodium: 29.3mg.

114. Lean, Mean, Green Machine Tropical Smoothie

Prep Time: 2 Mins
Total Time: 47 Mins
Ingredients
- 2 organic fairtrade bananas (fresh, medium)
- 0.5 cup "bremner's" pineapple (frozen)
- 0.5 cup "bremner's" mango (frozen)
- 1 cup "earthbound farm" baby spinach
- 1 packet "garden of life" "mangolicious" protein powder
- 1 cup water

Instructions
1. Blend in a high-speed blender and rejuvenate!

Nutritional Value
Protein: 11g Total Fat: 1g Total Carbohydrates: 43g
Sugar: 23g Sodium: 13mg

115. Orange And Pineapple Green Smoothie

Prep Time: 5 Mins
Total Time: 5 Mins
Ingredients
- 2 baby spinach, handfuls
- 2 naval oranges, small (peeled and seeded)
- Frozen pineapple chunks (slightly less than a ⅓ of a 16oz bag)
- Light coconut milk

Instructions
1. Place baby spinach and coconut milk into the blender and blend for a few seconds to break up the spinach.
2. Add in the oranges and frozen pineapple, then blend until completely smooth.
3. Enjoy!

Nutrition Information
Fat: 5.5g Carbohydrates: 23.3g Sugar: 16.9g Sodium: 26.8mg Fiber: 3.7g Protein: 1.7g

116. Green Protein Detox Smoothie

Prep Time: 3 Mins
Total Time: 3 Mins

Ingredients
- ½ cup unsweetened almond milk
- 1 tablespoon almond butter
- 1 banana
- 2 cups baby spinach

Instructions
1. Wash all the detox smoothie ingredients.
2. Add weight loss smoothie ingredients to the blender starting with the greens and ending with the fruit.
3. Blend until smooth, adding more water until you reach your desired green detox smoothie consistency.

Nutrition Value
Calories: 237 Fat: 11.4g Saturated Fat: 1g Fiber: 6.5g Protein: 6.9g Carbohydrates: 33.1

117. Glowing Green Detox Smoothie

Prep Time: 5 Mins
Total Time: 5 Mins

Ingredients
- 1 kiwi
- 1 banana
- ¼ cup pineapple
- 2 celery stalks
- 2 cups spinach
- 1 cup water

Instructions
1. Wash all the detox smoothie ingredients.
2. Add weight loss smoothie ingredients to the blender starting with the greens and ending with the fruit.
3. Blend until smooth, adding more water until you reach your desired green detox smoothie consistency.

Nutrition Value
Fat: 1.1g Saturated Fat: 0.2g Fiber: 7.8g Protein: 4.3g Carbohydrates: 46.7g

118. Peaches And Cream Oatmeal Green Smoothie

Prep Time: 2 Mins
Total Time: 2 Mins
Ingredients
- 1 cup frozen peach slices
- 1 cup greek yogurt i like unsweetened, but the peach flavor is excellent here
- ¼ cup oatmeal
- ¼ teaspoon vanilla extract
- 1 cup almond milk
- 1 cup baby spinach

Instructions
1. Add all of the ingredients to the blender.
2. Blend until smooth.
3. Serve.
4. Wash the blender immediately to avoid food sticking.

Nutritional Value
Fat: 4g Fiber: 5g Protein: 29g Carbohydrates: 46g

119. Berry Delicious Detox Diet Smoothie

Prep Time: 2 Mins
Total Time: 2 Mins
Ingredients
- ½ cup strawberries
- ½ cup blueberries
- ¼ cup raspberries
- 2 cups spinach

Instructions
1. Add all the ingredients to the blender and close.
2. Blend until smooth, adding more liquid as needed for desired consistency.
3. Pour into a glass or jar.
4. Clean out the blender right away to avoid sticking.

120. Kale And Apple Green Detox Smoothie

Prep Time: 5 Mins
Total Time: 5 Mins
Ingredients
- ⅔ cup almond milk unsweetened
- ¾ cup ice
- 1 ½ cups kale chopped
- 1 stalk celery chopped
- ½ red or green apple cored and chopped
- 1 tbsp ground flax seed
- 1 teaspoon honey optional

Instructions
1. Wash all the detox smoothie ingredients.
2. Add weight loss smoothie ingredients to the blender starting with the greens and ending with the fruit.
3. Blend until smooth, adding more water until you reach your desired green detox smoothie consistency.

Nutrition Value
Fat: 5.4g Saturated Fat: 0.3g Fiber: 4.5g Protein: 6g Carbohydrates: 17.5

121. Avocado Detox Smoothie

Total Time: 5 Mins
Ingredients
- 1 1/2 cups water
- 2 cups spinach or kale stemmed and chopped
- 1 apple unpeeled, cored and chopped
- 1/2 avocado chopped

Instructions
1. Wash all the detox smoothie ingredients.
2. Add weight loss smoothie ingredients to the blender starting with the greens and ending with the fruit.
3. Blend until smooth, adding more water until you reach your desired green detox smoothie consistency.

Nutrition Value
Calories: 335 Fat: 20.2g Saturated Fat: 4.2g Fiber: 13.5g Protein: 4.2g Carbohydrates: 41.6

122. Super Green Smoothie Bowl

Prep Time: 10 Minutes
Total Time: 10 Minutes

Ingredients
- Smoothie
- 1/4 ripe avocado
- 2 medium ripe bananas (previously sliced and frozen)
- 1 cup fresh or frozen mixed berries
- 2 large handfuls of spinach (organic when possible)
- 1 small handful kale (organic when possible/large stems removed)
- 1 1/2 - 2 cups unsweetened non-dairy milk store-bought
- 2 tbsp salted creamy almond or peanut butter
- Roasted unsalted sunflower seeds
- Granola
- Raw or roasted nuts (almonds, pecans, walnuts, etc.)
- Shredded unsweetened coconut
- Fresh berries
- Hemp seeds

Instructions
1. Add all smoothie ingredients to a blender and blend until creamy and smooth. Add more almond milk (or water) to thin.
2. Taste and adjust flavor as needed, adding more ripe banana (or maple syrup) for added sweetness, more spinach for a bright green hue, or almond milk for creaminess.
3. For the green smoothie, i used strawberries, which let the green color come through more. For the purple bowl, i used darker berries (raspberries, blackberries, blueberries).
4. For more protein, add nut butter! This also offsets/enhances the natural sweetness of the smoothie.
5. Divide between 2 serving bowls and top with desired toppings!
6. Best when fresh, though leftovers can be kept in jars in the fridge for up to 1-2 days.

Nutrition
Carbohydrates: 41.5g   Protein: 7.9g   Fat: 15.6g   Saturated Fat: 1.9g   Sodium: 171mg   Fiber: 9.5g   Sugar: 19 G

123. Simple Green Acai Smoothie

Prep Time: 5 Minutes
Total Time: 5 Minutes

Ingredients
- 1/2 pack of unsweetened sambazon frozen acai juice
- 2 very large handfuls of washed baby spinach
- 1 small banana or 2 tablespoons avocado (or half each)
- 3 tablespoons raw cashews (remember raw, no salt, not roasted & preferably organic)
- 1 cup purified water (plus more if needed)
- About a teaspoon of raw honey, to taste
- 4–5 ice cubes

Instructions
1. Blend all ingredients in a high-speed blender.
2. Serve immediately.

Nutritional Value
Protein: 2g   Carbohydrates: 19g   Dietary Fiber: 2g   Sugars: 14g   Fat: 1g   Sodium: 19mg

124. Healing Simple Green Smoothie

Prep Time: 5 Minutes
Total Time: 5 Minutes
Ingredients
- 1 1/2 cups kale (stems removed)
- 1/2 cup broccoli florets
- 1 cup water
- 1 green apple (halved and cored)
- 1/4 cup chopped avocado
- Juice of 1 lemon
- Dash of ground pepper

Instructions
1. Blend the kale, broccoli, and water until smooth.
2. Add the apple, avocado, lemon juice, and red pepper, and blend again.

Nutritional Facts
Protein: 1.6g Carbohydrates: 21.2g Fat: 0.5g Sodium 29.3mg.

125. The Lean Green Lime Machine

Prep Time: 5 Min
Total Time: 10 Min
Ingredients
- 2 cucumbers, rinsed and cut into medium-size pieces. I leave the skin on and buy organic cucumbers when possible.
- A handful of fresh mint leaves
- 2 tsp fresh root ginger
- 2 handfuls of baby spinach leaves
- 1 lime, peeled and halved

Instructions
1. Prepare the ingredients and process them through the juicer, as instructed.
2. Serve chilled in a tall glass or jar with a couple of ice cubes.

126. Weight Loss Green Smoothie

Total Time: 20 Mins
Ingredients
- 1-2 handfuls green grapes (seedless)
- 1 whole apple (quartered)
- 1 whole pear (quartered)
- 2 handfuls spinach leaves
- 2 leaves kale
- 1 tbsp chia seeds
- 1-2 cup ice cubes

Instructions
1. Put all the ingredients into the vitamix container in the order listed and secure the lid.
2. Select speed 1, turn the machine on and quickly increase to the highest speed.
3. Use the tamper to effectively press the ingredients into the blades if required whilst processing.
4. Blend for 60-90 seconds or until desired consistency is reached.
5. Stop the machine and serve.

127. Lean Green Peach Smoothie

Prep Time: 4 Minutes
Ingredients
- 1 cup silk almond milk unsweetened vanilla
- 2 cups spinach fresh
- 1 green apple cored and seeds removed
- 2 cups peaches frozen, sliced
- 1-2 tbsp ground flaxseed
- 1 frozen banana optional

Instructions
1. Combine all ingredients in a high-speed blender and blend for 1-2 minutes until smooth, scraping down the sides if needed.
2. Divide mixture into two glasses and enjoy immediately.

Nutrition Value
Carbohydrates: 43g Protein: 4g Fat: 4g Saturated Fat: 1g Sodium: 189mg Potassium: 797mg Fiber: 8g Sugar: 30g Calcium: 203mg Iron: 2mg

128. The Best Green Smoothie

Prep Time: 5 Minutes
Total Time: 5 Minutes

Ingredients
- 1 cup frozen pineapple chunks
- ½ cup frozen mango chunks
- 1/2 medium ripe avocado
- 1 inch knob of ginger, peeled
- 2 cups organic spinach
- 1 cup unsweetened almond milk, plus more as necessary

Instructions
1. In a large high-powered blender, add in all ingredients and blend on high for 1-2 minutes or until all ingredients are well combined.
2. If necessary, add in more milk to thin the smoothie and blend again.

Nutrition Value
Fat: 16.8g Saturated Fat: 1.9g Carbohydrates: 40.6g Fiber: 10.9g Sugar: 22.8g Protein: 5.5g

129. Low-Carb Green Smoothie

Prep Time: 5 Minutes
Total Time: 5 Minutes

Ingredients
- 1 medium avocado - peeled and pitted
- 1 cup spinach
- 1 1/2 cups unsweetened coconut milk
- 1 scoop of sugar-free vanilla protein powder
- 1 tbsp peanut butter powder
- 1 tbsp freshly squeezed lemon juice

Instructions
1. Add all the ingredients to a blender and puree for about 30 seconds.
2. Taste to adjust flavor and serve immediately.

Nutritional Value
Carbohydrates: 7g Protein: 6g Fat: 14g Saturated Fat: 4g Polyunsaturated Fat: 1g Monounsaturated Fat: 8g Cholesterol: 1mg Sodium: 84mg Potassium: 480mg Fiber: 7g Sugar: 1g

130. Lean Green Protein Juice

Prep Time: 10 Mins
Ingredients
- 1 green apple
- 1 lemon
- 1/4 " piece of ginger
- 4 cups spinach leaves
- 1/2 an english cucumber
- 2 celery stalks

Instructions
1. Start with chilled produce.
2. Chop all ingredients into 1" pieces and add them one at a time to your hurom slow juicer (or similar), starting with an ingredient that isn't as juicy (like spinach), and alternating with an ingredient that makes lots of juice (like apple).
3. This will ensure that the juicy ingredients flush the not-so-juicy ingredients through the juicer and you'll get more of them in your cup!
4. Serve over ice, and garnish with a celery stalk, slice of lemon or cucumber, and enjoy!

131. Green Smoothie For Beginners

Prep Time: 5 Mins
Total Time: 5 Mins
Ingredients
- 2 cups spinach
- 1 banana peeled & sliced
- ½ cup strawberries frozen
- ½ cup mango peeled & cubed
- ½ cup soymilk
- 1 stalk celery peeled & sliced (optional)

Instructions
1. Add ingredients in blender. Blend well. Enjoy.

Nutritional Facts
Fat: 3.3g Sat Fat: 0.5g Sodium: 126mg Carbohydrate: 55.2g Fiber: 8.2g Sugar: 34.6g Protein: 8.3 Calcium: 123mg Iron: 3mg Potassium: 1195mg

SALADS

132. Tabouleh

Prep Time: 30 Mins
Total Time: 30 Mins

Ingredients
- 3 bunches fresh parsley i prefer curly
- 2/3 cup lemon juice
- 1/3 cup olive oil
- 1 teaspoon kosher salt
- 1 teaspoon pepper
- 1/2 cup cracked bulgur dry (can substitute for 1 1/2 cup cooked/cooled quinoa, or 1 1/2 cup minced cauliflower)
- 2 cloves garlic minced
- 1/2 sweet onion minced
- 3 tomatoes deseeded, minced

Instructions
1. If you have time, thoroughly rinse the parsley (3 bunches) the night before. Wrap it in paper towels and place it in the fridge. This will make the tabouleh extra crisp! If you don't have time to rinse the night before, be sure to get the parsley as dry as possible.
2. In a small bowl, combine olive oil (1/3 cup), lemon juice (2/3 cup), salt (1 teaspoon) and pepper (1 teaspoon).
3. Add cracked bulgur (1/2 cup) to the lemon juice/olive oil and let it sit for 30 minutes – 1 hour, depending on how soft you want the bulgur to be.
4. Pick the leaves from the stems of the parsley. I do this by grabbing the bunch of parsley and sliding a sharp knife over the top, then picking out any large stems.
5. Place leaves into the food processor. Pulse the parsley until it is finely chopped using 1 second intervals. Make sure not to pulse too much! Alternatively you can use a knife to chop the parsley.
6. Add minced sweet onion (1/2), minced tomatoes (3 deseeded), minced garlic (2 cloves) and parsley to the bulgur and stir to combine.
7. Add more salt/pepper to taste. Tabouleh is best served after resting in the fridge overnight. Enjoy!

Nutritional Value
Calories: 312kcal Carbohydrates: 34g Protein: 6g Fat: 19g Fiber: 8g Sugar: 6g Net Carbs: 26g

133. Low Carb Potato Salad

Prep Time: 30 Mins
Total Time: 30 Mins

Ingredients
- 2 lbs radishes raw
- 8 slices bacon
- 4 eggs
- 5 scallions chopped
- 1/2 cup celery diced
- 2 tablespoons dill chopped, fresh
- 2/3 cup regular mayonnaise
- 2 tablespoon mustard
- 1 teaspoon kosher salt
- 1/2 teaspoon black pepper

Instructions
1. Add raw radishes (2 pounds) to a pot of water and bring to a boil.
2. Boil, uncovered, for 15 minutes, or until a fork inserted into the center feels tender.

3. In another pot, add eggs (4), cover with water and bring to a boil.
4. Once boiling, cover with a lid and remove from heat. Cook for 18 minutes while you prep the remaining ingredients.
5. Meanwhile, cook the bacon (8 slices).
6. Allow bacon to cool on a paper towel-lined plate, then crumble into small pieces.
7. Once radishes are cooked, drain them and remove as much liquid as possible.
8. Once eggs have cooked and cooled, peel and dice them.
9. Add cooked bacon, radishes, eggs, diced celery (1/2 cup) and chopped scallions (5) to a large bowl.
10. In a small bowl, combine regular mayonnaise (2/3 cup), mustard (2 tablespoons), chopped fresh dill (2 tablespoons), salt (1 teaspoon) and black pepper (1/2 teaspoon).
11. Pour dressing over the salad ingredients, and toss until everything is thoroughly coated.
12. Place salad in the fridge, allowing the ingredients to marry until you're ready to serve. Enjoy!

Nutrition Value
Calories: 275kcal Carbohydrates: 5g Protein: 7g Fat: 25g Cholesterol: 104mg Fiber: 2g Sugar: 3g Net Carbs: 3g

134. The Lean Green Kale Bowl

Prep Time: 15 Mins
Cook Time: 5 Mins
Total Time: 20 Mins

Ingredients
- 2 large handfuls of kale
- A handful of mint leaves
- ½ lemon, juiced
- ½ tablespoon olive oil
- ½ head broccoli, chopped into thin florets
- 4 eggs
- 1 avocado, flesh scooped out
- 35g almonds, toasted and coarsely chopped
- Salt + pepper to taste

Dressing
- 50g goat's feta
- ½ tablespoon olive oil
- 2-3 tablespoons water
- Salt + pepper to taste

Instructions
1. Start by making your dressing. Simply add all the ingredients into a small blender or food processor and blitz until smooth and runny. If you'd like a more creamy dressing to add 2 tablespoons of water, and for a more sauce-y one, add 3 tablespoons. Taste, adjust seasoning and set aside until ready to drizzle.
2. Shred your kale leaves and add to a large bowl with mint, lemon juice, and ½ tablespoon olive oil. If you're having your broccoli raw, add it now as well.
3. Toss everything together, massaging the kale as it starts to get softer and more tender.
4. Divide into two bowls and set aside while you make the rest of the salad.
5. If you're not having your broccoli raw, boil some water in a pan and place a steamer basket with your broccoli on it.
6. Steam for about 2-3 minutes, just until slightly tender but still with a bite.
7. Remove from the pan and set aside to cool and then toss with the kale salad.
8. Add your eggs to the pan with the boiling water and boil until your desired done-ness. 3-4 minutes for soft, and 5-6 minutes for the set. Carefully drain the water and run the eggs under cold water to stop the cooking process.
9. Once they're cool enough to handle, peel and add to the bowl with the kale salad.
10. Place each half of the avocado in each bowl, sprinkle over the almonds, some salt + pepper, and drizzle the dressing.

Nutritional Facts
Carbohydrates: 61g Protein: 11g Fat: 2g Saturated Fat: 0g Cholesterol: 0mg Sodium: 410mg Potassium: 2224mg Fiber: 11g Sugar: 10g

135. Cauliflower Tabbouleh

Prep Time: 30 Mins
Total Time: 30 Mins
Ingredients
- 2/3 cup lemon juice
- 1/3 cup olive oil
- 1 clove garlic minced
- 1 teaspoon kosher salt
- 1/2 teaspoon pepper
- 2 1/2 cups cauliflower rice
- 5 bunches fresh parsley thoroughly rinsed! I recommend rinsing the night before and storing it in the fridge in clean kitchen towels.
- 1 small red onion minced
- 12 ounces cherry tomatoes quartered

Instructions
1. In a large bowl, combine olive oil (1/3 cup), lemon juice (2/3 cup), salt (1 teaspoon) and pepper (1/2 teaspoon).
2. In a food processor, process cauliflower (2 1/2 cups) until it's a fine grain, similar to the size of bulgur grain, using 1-second intervals. Place the cauliflower in the lemon juice/olive oil and let it sit white prepping the remaining ingredients.
3. Pick the leaves from the stems of the parsley (5 bunches). To save time, drag a sharp knife over the top of a parsley bunch while holding the stems, then remove any large stems from the leaves (you won't notice the small stems).
4. Place leaves into the food processor, and pulse until finely chopped (make sure not to overprocess!).
5. Add quartered cherry tomatoes (12 ounces), parsley, and minced red onions (1 small) to the cauliflower bowl, and stir to thoroughly combine.
6. Taste and adjust seasoning to your liking (i usually add an additional teaspoon of salt). Chill in the fridge for 1 hour-overnight before serving, and enjoy!

Nutrition Value
Calories: 161kcal Carbohydrates: 12g Protein: 3g Fat: 13g Fiber: 3g Sugar: 4g Net carbs: 9g

136. The Ultimate Wedge Salad Recipe

Prep Time: 15 Minutes
Cook Time: 5 Minutes
Total Time: 20 Minutes
Ingredients
For The Blue Cheese Dressing:
- ½ cup sour cream
- ½ cup mayonnaise
- 1/3 cup buttermilk
- 1 tablespoon apple cider vinegar
- ½ teaspoon salt
- ¼ teaspoon cracked black pepper
- ¼ teaspoon garlic powder
- ½ cup crumbled blue cheese

For The Wedge Salad:
- 8 slices bacon chopped
- 1 head iceberg lettuce
- 1 cup cherry or grape tomatoes halved
- 1 cup blue cheese dressing
- ½ cup chopped scallions
- ½ cup crumbled blue cheese

Instructions

1. **Make The Dressing:** set out a medium mixing bowl. Add the sour cream, mayonnaise, buttermilk, apple cider vinegar, salt, pepper, and garlic powder. Stir well. Then mix in the crumbled blue cheese. Cover and chill until ready to use. (if possible, make a day ahead, or early in the day, so the blue cheese has time to permeate the dressing.)
2. **Cook The Bacon:** set a skillet over medium heat. Place the chopped bacon in the skillet. Brown the bacon for 4-6 minutes until crispy, stirring regularly. Then scoop the bacon out of the skillet onto a paper towel-lined plate to drain off the grease.
3. **Prep The Veggies:** slice the tomatoes in half and chop the scallions. Then set the head of lettuce on the cutting board. Trim the root/core end a little. Cut the head in half, through the core. (this helps hold the wedges together.) Then cut each half in two, through the core.
4. **Stack The Wedges:** set each lettuce wedge on a plate. Drizzle with a generous amount of blue cheese dressing. (at least ¼ cup per salad.) Then sprinkle the tops with halved tomatoes, scallions, bacon, and more blue cheese crumbles. Finish each salad plate off with a bit of fresh cracked pepper. Serve cold.

Nutritional Facts

Calories: 653kcal Carbohydrates: 12g Protein: 19g Fat: 59g Saturatedfat: 21g Cholesterol: 84mg Sodium: 1870mg Potassium: 547mg Fiber: 2g Sugar: 8g

137.	Spring Green Salad

Prep Time: 10 Minutes
Cook Time: 15 Minutes
Total Time: 25 Minutes

Ingredients
Dressing:
- Zest of half a lemon
- 2 tablespoons fresh lemon juice
- 1 teaspoon honey warmed until in liquid form
- 1/2 teaspoon dijon mustard
- 1/2 teaspoon kosher salt
- 3 tablespoons avocado oil or olive oil

Salad:
- 1/2 cup shelled roasted and salted pistachios
- 10 asparagus stalks
- 1/2 cup frozen peas
- 8 leaves green leaf lettuce about half a large head

Instructions

1. Measure out the dressing ingredients with measuring spoons and pour them into a small- or medium-sized bowl, beating them together swiftly with a whisk until well combined.
2. Alternatively, you could pour all the ingredients into a small mason jar, seal it, and shake to combine. Once done, set aside.
3. If the pistachios aren't already shelled, do that first as it will take the most time. To do so, simply pry apart the shell with your fingers. Otherwise, move on to cooking the asparagus.
4. In a large pot, pour in about an inch of water and place a steamer basket into the pot but above the water. Place the pot over medium heat to bring to a boil. Once boiling, turn down the heat to medium-low to maintain a simmer.
5. While you wait for the water to boil, prep the asparagus. Wash the asparagus, then using a large sharp knife and cutting board, cut off between 1.5 to 2 inches of the thicker, woody end of the asparagus. Then cut them into roughly 1 inch pieces.
6. Put the asparagus in the basket and cover, cooking for 5 minutes or until asparagus is bright green and slightly tender.
7. While asparagus is cooking, cook the frozen peas according to package directions, typically pouring a small amount of water into a small pot and cooking for 4 to 5 minutes, covered, over medium heat. Drain and set aside when peas are done cooking.
8. Once asparagus is cooked, remove it (still in the steamer basket) and run it under cold water for 10 to 15 seconds to keep it from over cooking. Then drain and set aside.
9. Wash the lettuce leaves, dry them off with a towel or in a salad spinner, then cut them into pieces with the large sharp knife and cutting board. Alternatively, you can tear them up into small pieces. Place them in a

large bowl. Put the pistachios, peas, and asparagus in with the lettuce.
10. Whisk the dressing again if it separated, then pour half the dressing over the lettuce mixture. Toss with a pair of tongs (or other utensils) to combine. If you like more dressing on your salad, pour remaining dressing over the lettuce mixture and toss to combine again. Serve immediately.

Nutrition Value
Calories: 143kcal Carbohydrates: 8g Protein: 4g Fat: 12g Saturated Fat: 1g Sodium: 205mg Potassium: 233mg Fiber: 3g Sugar: 3g

138. Detox Salad

Total Time: 15 Minutes

Ingredients
- White balsamic vinaigrette salad dressing ingredients:
- 2 tablespoons white balsamic vinegar
- 1 tablespoon red wine vinegar
- 1 tablespoon dijon mustard
- 1 clove garlic minced/grated
- 1/4 cup extra virgin olive oil
- Pink himalayan salt and black pepper to taste

Detox Kale Salad Ingredients:
- 3 cups finely chopped kale leaves stems removed before chopping, about 5-6 large leaves
- 2 cups finely chopped broccoli florets
- 2 cups finely chopped red cabbage
- 1 cup cilantro chopped then measured
- 1 cup shredded carrots
- 1/2 cup chopped walnuts
- 3 stalks green onion chopped (both green and white parts), about 1/3 cup
- 2 radishes thinly sliced
- 1 avocado skin and pit removed, and diced

Instructions
1. **Make The Salad Dressing:** In a mason jar or bowl, grate the garlic into the jar. Add the olive oil, balsamic vinegar, red wine vinegar, and mustard. Cover with a lid (or mix in a bowl). Sprinkle with a dash of salt and pepper to taste. Set aside until ready to use.
2. **Make The Salad:** Remove the leaves of the kale leaves from the stem. Add to a food processor and pulse until finely chopped. Transfer to a large serving or mixing bowl or set aside. Repeat and chop the broccoli and red cabbage. Set aside. Chop and dice the cilantro, green onion, walnuts, radishes and avocado.
3. In a large serving plate or mixing bowl add the prepared kale, broccoli, cabbage, carrots, cilantro, green onion, walnuts, radishes and avocado. Top with the dressing and toss to coat until the ingredients are mixed. Season with salt and pepper to taste. Serve right away.

Nutrition Value
Carbohydrates: 23g Protein: 8g Fat: 31g Saturated Fat: 4g Sodium: 121mg Potassium: 964mg Fiber: 8g Sugar: 6g Calcium: 157mg Iron: 3mg

139. Healthy Taco Salad Recipe

Prep Time: 5minutes
Cook Time: 10minutes
Total Time: 15minutes

Ingredients
- 1 lb ground beef
- 1 tsp avocado oil (or any oil of choice)
- 2 tbsp taco seasoning (store-bought or home-made)

- 8 oz romaine lettuce (chopped)
- 1 1/3 cup grape tomatoes (halved)
- 3/4 cup cheddar cheese (shredded)
- 1 medium avocado (cubed)
- 1/2 cup green onions (chopped)
- 1/3 cup salsa
- 1/3 cup sour cream

Instructions

1. Heat oil in a skillet over high heat. Add ground beef. Stir fry, breaking up the pieces with a spatula, for about 7-10 minutes, until the beef is browned and moisture has evaporated.
2. Stir taco seasoning into the ground beef until well combined.
3. Meanwhile, combine all remaining ingredients in a large bowl. Add the ground beef. Toss everything together.

Nutrition Facts

Fat: 25g Protein: 20g Total Carbs: 9g Net Carbs: 5g Fiber: 4g Sugar: 2g

140. Simple Kale Spinach Salad With Avocado Green Goddess Dressing

Prep Time: 10 Mins
Total Time: 10 Mins

Ingredients

For The Salad

- 2 cups spinach
- 2 cups chopped kale, massaged with olive oil
- 1 pint cherry tomatoes, halved
- 1 tbs hemp hearts

Green Goddess Dressing

- 3/4 cup water
- 1/4 cup extra virgin olive oil
- 1 1/2 medium avocados (or 2 small), pitted and fleshed
- 1/2 cup fresh basil leaves (a small handful)
- 2 tbs tahini
- 1 tbs apple cider vinegar
- 1 tsp minced garlic
- 1/2 tsp pink salt, to taste

Instructions

1. Toss spinach and kale in large bowl, top with cherry tomatoes and hemp hearts. Set aside.
2. In a small blender or food processor add all of your dressing ingredients–if using a nutribullet it helps if you add the ingredients in the order above–and process until smooth. Dressing is pretty thick, so if you want it thinner you can add more water 1-2 tablespoons at a time.
3. Toss dressing with salad, or serve individually. Enjoy!

Nutrition Information

Calories: 210 Sugar: 2g Sodium: 176mg Fat: 19saturated Fat: 3g Unsaturated Fat: 12g Carbohydrates: 9 Fiber: 5g Protein: 5g

141. Lean Beef Taco Salad

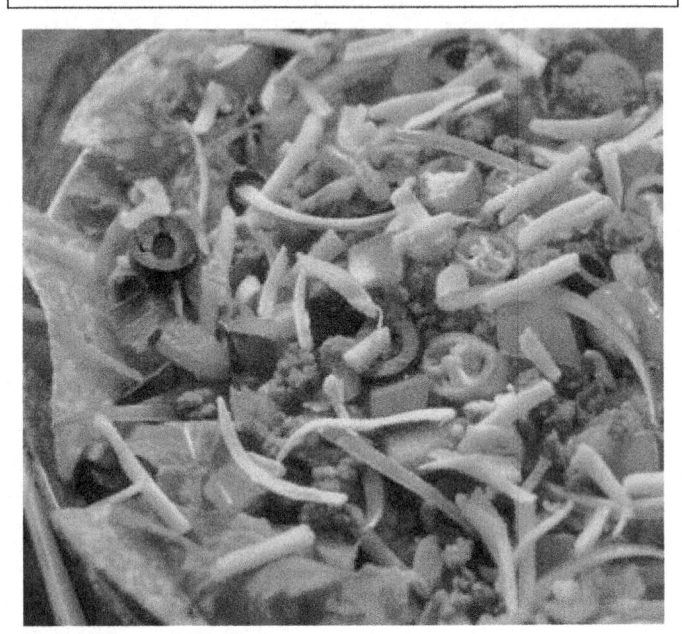

Total Time: 30 Minutes

Ingredient

- 1 lb (500 g) extra lean ground beef
- 1 cup (250 ml) water
- 12 cups (3 l) torn romaine or iceberg lettuce
- 1 can (19 fl oz/ 540 ml) pinto beans, rinsed, drained
- 1 1/2 cups (375 ml) chopped tomatoes
- 3 tbsp (45 ml) sliced green onions
- 3/4 cup (175 ml) shredded reduced-fat old cheddar cheese

- ¾ cup (175 ml) old el paso thick n' chunky salsa (any variety)
- 3/4 cup (175 ml) fat free sour cream
- 1/4 cup (50 ml) baked tortilla chips (optional)

Instructions
1. In large nonstick skillet, cook beef over medium-high heat 5 to 7 minutes, stirring frequently, until thoroughly cooked; drain.
2. Stir in water and taco seasoning mix; reduce heat to medium-low.
3. Cook about 5 minutes or until most of liquid has evaporated.
4. Divide lettuce among 6 salad plates; top each with meat mixture and remaining ingredients except chips.
5. Arrange chips around salad. Serve immediately.

Nutritional Facts
Carbohydrates: 10g Protein: 15g Fat: 8g Saturated Fat: 1g Cholesterol: 61mg Sodium: 349mg Potassium: 589mg Fiber: 3g Sugar: 5g

142. Avocado Chicken Salad

Prep Time: 15 Minutes
Cook Time: 5 Minutes
Total Time: 20 Minutes

Ingredients
- 2 medium cooked chicken breasts shredded or chopped (we used rotisserie chicken)
- 2 ripe avocados pitted and diced
- 1/2 cup corn roasted, canned, or frozen
- 1/4 cup red or green onion minced
- 2 tablespoons cilantro minced (or parsley or dill)
- 2 tablespoons lime or lemon juice
- 2 tablespoons olive oil
- Salt and pepper to taste

Instructions
1. In a large bowl, add the shredded chicken, avocado, onion, avocados, corn, and cilantro.
2. Drizzle with lime (or lemon) juice, olive oil, and season with salt and pepper. Toss gently until all the ingredients are combined.

Nutrition Facts
Carbohydrates: 9g Protein: 20g Fat: 17g Saturated Fat: 3g Cholesterol: 49mg Sodium: 48mg Potassium: 509mg Fiber: 5g Sugar: 1g Calcium: 17mg Iron: 1mg

Prep time: 15 minutes
Total time: 15 minutes

Ingredients
- 1 lb 3 cups cooked chicken, cubed
- 3/4 cup 3 large celery stalks, diced
- 1/4 cup red onion finely chopped
- 1/4 cup parsley or dill finely chopped (optional)
- 1 cup pecans, almonds or cashews
- 1/2 cup plain yogurt 2+% fat
- 1/4 cup mayo i used avocado oil mayo
- 2 tsp dijon mustard
- 1 tsp any vinegar except balsamic
- 1/2 tsp salt
- Ground black pepper to taste

Instructions
1. In a small skillet, add pecans and toast on low-medium heat until fragrant and brown-ish, stirring often. Transfer to a cutting board, let cool a bit and chop coarsely.

2. In a medium bowl, add toasted pecans, chicken, celery, onion, parsley, yogurt, mayo, mustard, vinegar, salt and pepper. Stir gently to mix and adjust salt to taste if necessary.
3. Refrigerate for at least 2 hours as salad tastes best cold.
4. Serve with greens, quinoa, brown rice or make a chicken salad sandwich with whole wheat bread.

Nutrition Value
Carbohydrates: 2g Protein: 8g Fat: 16g Saturated Fat: 3g Cholesterol: 32mg Sodium: 173mg Potassium: 149mg Fiber: 1g Sugar: 1g Calcium: 27mg Iron: 1mg

143.	Ultimate Garden Salad Recipe

Prep Time: 20 Mins
Cook Time: 3 Mins
Total Time: 20 Mins
Ingredients
Garden salad dressing
- 1/4 cup olive oil
- 2 tbsp balsamic vinegar
- 1 tbsp lemon juice
- 1/2 tsp black pepper
- 1/2 tsp salt

Garden salad
- 1 lb mixed greens
- 1 avocado
- 4 cucumbers
- 3 tomatoes
- 2 green onions
- 1/4 cup crumbled feta cheese

Instructions
1. Combine oil, balsamic vinegar, lemon juice, salt and pepper together by whisking with a fork. Set aside.
2. Dressing mixed in a bowl with a spoon
3. Prepare all the veggies and feta cheese for the salad.
4. A bowl with mixed greens, 3 tomatoes, 4 cucumbers, an avocado, green onions and feta on the table
5. Place leafy greens on the bottom, top it off with the rest of the ingredients.
6. Ultimate garden salad ingredients in a bowl
7. Drizzle the dressing right before serving the salad and toss everything together. You can sprinkle some extra feta on top. It's best served right away.
8. Ultimate garden salad in a bowl

Nutrition Facts
Fat: 15g Saturated Fat: 2g Cholesterol: 5mg Sodium: 294mg Potassium: 727mg Carbohydrates: 13g Fiber: 4g Sugar: 5g Protein: 4g Calcium: 82mg Iron: 1.5mg

144.	Medifast Lean And Green Recipe

Prep Time: 8 Minutes
Cook Time: 22 Minutes
Total Time: 30 Minutes
Ingredients
- 4- oz lean ground hamburger
- Oz shredded cheddar cheese
- 1 ¼ cup broccoli cut into bite-sized pieces
- ¼ cup rotel tomatoes
- ¼ teaspoon garlic powder
- ¼ teaspoon onion powder
- ¼ teaspoon salt divided
- Pinch of red pepper flakes
- 2 tablespoons low sodium chicken stock

Instructions

1. Put your broccoli in a bowl with your chicken stock and cover with plastic wrap. Put in the microwave for 4 minutes, or until tender and cooked.
2. In a large skillet brown your hamburger and drain the grease if needed when it's done.
3. Add your rotel tomatoes, garlic powder, onion powder, salt, and red pepper flakes and stir well.
4. When your broccoli is finished cooking then add it to your skillet and toss with the hamburger mixture.
5. Add everything to a bowl and top with your shredded cheddar cheese.

Nutritional Facts
Carbohydrates: 35g Protein: 21g Fat: 25g Saturated fat: 14g Cholesterol: 83mg Sodium: 388mg Potassium: 264mg Fiber: 1g Sugar: 2g Calcium: 337mg Iron: 1mg

145. Healthy Lunch Salad

Prep time: 10 mins
Total time: 10 mins

Ingredients
- 4-5 leaves romaine lettuce, chopped (use romaine hearts)
- 2 cremini mushrooms, chopped
- 4 grape tomatoes, quartered
- ⅓ zucchini, chopped
- ⅛ c. Roasted/unsalted sunflower seeds
- ¼ c. Shredded cheddar cheese
- ⅛ tsp. Ground black pepper
- 2 tsp. Dressing (1 tsp. Extra virgin olive oil + 1 tsp. Apple cider vinegar)

Instructions
1. Clean each vegetable well.
2. Chop all veggies and place into a bowl (or pyrex container to take to work!)
3. Add the pepper and dressing, then toss to mix in well.
4. Enjoy!

Nutrition Information
Fat: 21.9g Carbohydrates: 12.8g Sugar: 2.4g Sodium: 199mg Fiber: 3.8g Protein: 13.7g

146. Asian-Style Tuna Salad Recipe

Total Time: 10 Minutes

Ingredients
- 10 oz canned tuna in water
- 5 tbsp avocado oil mayonnaise
- 1 tbsp dijon mustard
- 1 tbsp lime juice
- 1 tbsp gluten-free soy sauce
- 2 tsp sesame oil
- 1 tbsp sriracha
- 1 tbsp black sesame seeds
- 2 green onions
- 1 large carrot
- 1 large stalk
- Celery
- ½ cucumber
- ½ tsp garlic powder
- ½ tsp kosher salt
- ½ tsp black pepper
- 2 heads bibb lettuce

Instructions
1. Slice green onions, dice carrot, celery, and cucumber.
2. Drain tuna. Transfer the meat to a large bowl. Break tuna apart with a fork.

3. Add mayonnaise, mustard, lime juice, soy sauce, sesame oil, sesame seeds, and sriracha to tuna and stir to fully incorporate.
4. Add chopped veggies, and mix again.
5. Transfer tuna salad to bibb lettuce and enjoy!
6. Optional: garnish with extra sriracha and sesame seeds

Nutritional Facts
Carbs: 5g Fat: 20g Protein: 20g

147. Salmon Salad

Prep Time: 5 Mins
Cook Time: 10 Mins
Total Time: 15 Mins

Ingredients
- 6-7 oz salmon (i used 1.5 salmon burgers from costco)
- 1 cup green beans
- ⅓ small avocado
- 4 kalamata olives
- Salt and pepper
- ½ tomatoes
- 1 tbsp feta
- Olive oil

Instructions
1. Steam or pressure cook green beans until just tender
2. Cook salmon and cut into pieces
3. Sauté tomatoes in a non stick pan with a little olive oil and spices. Add salmon
4. Plate green beans, add tomatoes and salmon, avocado and sprinkle with feta.

Nutrition Facts
Protein: 29.5g; Carbohydrates: 34.3g; Dietary Fiber: 7g; Fat: 21.9g; Saturated Fat: 3.4g; Calcium: 93.1mg; Iron: 2.7mg; Sodium: 791.7mg; Sugar: 2g; Calories From Fat: 197kcal.

148. Simple Taco Salad

Prep Time: 20 Minutes
Total Time: 20 Minutes

Ingredients
- 1 pound ground round beef (85% lean)
- 1 can (16 oz each) beans in chili seasoned sauce
- 1 teaspoon chili powder
- 1 can (10 oz each) original diced tomatoes & green chilies, drained, liquid reserved
- 6 cups chopped romaine lettuce
- 1 cup shredded cheddar cheese
- 1-1/2 cups broken tortilla chips

Instructions
1. Cook beef in large skillet over medium-high heat 7 minutes or until crumbled and no longer pink, stirring occasionally; drain. Add chili beans, chili powder and reserved liquid from tomatoes. Cook 2 minutes or until hot; set aside.
2. Divide lettuce between 4 serving plates. Spoon meat mixture evenly over lettuce. Top evenly with cheese, broken chips and drained tomatoes.

149. Skinny Chicken Salad

Total Time: 10 Minutes
Ingredients
- 4 ounces shredded or diced (cooked) boneless, skinless, chicken breast (abt 1 cup)
- 1/4 cup diced celery
- 2 tablespoons sliced green onion
- 1/4 cup diced sweet, crisp apple
- 1 tablespoon light mayo
- 1 tablespoon light sour cream or greek yogurt
- Optional: 1/2-1 tablespoon chopped fresh parsley or cilantro
- 1/8 teaspoon curry powder
- 1/4 teaspoon red wine vinegar
- 1 tablespoon toasted sliced almonds
- Salt and pepper to taste

Instructions
1. Combine all ingredients except almonds and stir to combine. If possible, chill for an hour or so before eating.
2. Before serving, mix in almonds.
3. Eat-in a lettuce wrap, on whole-grain bread, in a wrap, or a pita.

Nutritional Info
Cal: 267g Protein: 28g Fat: 12g Carbs: 8g Fiber: 2g Sugar: 6 G

150. Lean Green Chicken Pesto Pasta

Prep Time: 15 Minutes
Total Time: 30 Minutes
Ingredients
- Kale pesto
- 3 cups (48g) raw kale (stems removed)
- 2 cup (12g) fresh basil
- 2 tablespoons (28g) olive oil
- 3 tablespoons lemon juice
- 3 garlic cloves
- ¼ teaspoon salt
- Pasta salad
- 2 cups (280g) cooked chicken breast (diced)
- 6 oz (176g) uncooked "barilla" rotini chickpea pasta
- 1 cup (20g) arugula or baby spinach
- 3oz (84g) "bel gioioso" fresh mozzarella (diced)
- Optional: additional basil leaves or red pepper flakes for garnish

Instructions
1. Make the pesto by adding the kale, basil, olive oil, garlic cloves, lemon juice, and salt to a food processor. Blend until smooth. Season to taste with additional salt and pepper.
2. Cook pasta according to package directions. Strain, reserving ¼ cup cooking liquid.
3. In a large bowl, mix the cooked pasta, diced chicken, pesto, arugula or spinach, reserved pasta liquid, and mozzarella and toss until combined. Sprinkle with extra chopped basil or red pepper flakes (if desired).
4. Serve chilled or warm. This pasta salad is delicious on its own, as a salad mix-in, or as a side! Store leftovers

in an airtight container in the refrigerator for 3-5 days. Enjoy!

Nutrition Facts
Carbs: 22.5g Protein: 10.5g Fat: 10g

151. Easy Healthy Taco Salad Recipe With Ground Beef

Prep Time: 10 Minutes
Cook Time: 10 Minutes
Total Time: 20 Minutes

Ingredients
- 1 lb ground beef
- 1 tsp avocado oil (or any oil of choice)
- 2 tbsp taco seasoning (store-bought or home-made)
- 8 oz romaine lettuce (chopped)
- 1 1/3 cup grape tomatoes (halved)
- 3/4 cup cheddar cheese (shredded)
- 1 medium avocado (cubed)
- 1/2 cup green onions (chopped)
- 1/3 cup salsa
- 1/3 cup sour cream

Instructions
1. Heat oil in a skillet over high heat. Add ground beef. Stir fry, breaking up the pieces with a spatula, for about 7-10 minutes, until the beef is browned and moisture has evaporated.
2. Stir taco seasoning into the ground beef until well combined.
3. Meanwhile, combine all remaining ingredients in a large bowl. Add the ground beef. Toss everything together.

Nutrition Facts

Calories: 332 Fat: 25g Protein: 20g Total Carbs: 9g
Net Carbs: 5g Fiber: 4g Sugar: 2g

152. High-Protein Chicken Salad

Prep Time: 10 Minutes

Ingredients
- 1 lb cooked chicken breast or rotisserie chicken, shredded
- 1/2 cup red onion, diced
- 1/2 cup sweet apple, diced (red or green)
- 2/3 cup grapes, quartered or halved (red or white)
- 2/3 cup dried cranberries (or craisins)
- 1/2 cup chopped walnuts (or nut of choice)
- 2/3 cup plain 2% greek yogurt
- 2 tbsp fresh lemon juice (or more to taste)
- 1/2 tsp garlic powder
- Salt & pepper
- 6 medium lettuce leaves

Instructions
1. In a large bowl, combine all ingredients. Mix until well combined.
2. Using a 3/4 cup measuring scoop, portion out the chicken salad onto lettuce leaves.

Nutrition Facts

Carbohydrates: 2g Protein: 19g Fat: 21g Saturated Fat: 7g Polyunsaturated Fat: 4g Monounsaturated Fat: 3g Cholesterol: 66mg Sodium: 380mg Potassium: 60mg Sugar: 1g Calcium: 100mg Iron: 2mg

153. Creamy Cucumber Salad

Prep Time: 25 Minutes
Total Time: 25 Minutes

Ingredients
- 2 english cucumbers
- 1/4 cup finely chopped red onion
- 1/4 cup chopped dill
- 1/3 cup sour cream
- 1/3 cup plain unsweetened yogurt
- 1 tbsp white wine vinegar
- 1/2 tbsp honey - optional, leave out for keto, without honey 9g carbs (8 net)
- 1-2 tsp sea salt
- Pepper

Instructions
1. Wash cucumbers and peel lengthwise in zebra patterns
2. Use a mandoline to slice the cucumbers into about 1-2 mm thick rounds into a large bowl.
3. Add sea salt to the cucumber slices and mix well with your hands, then set them aside in the bowl for at least 15 minutes (up to 30) until they release most of their water.
4. In the meantime, finely chop red onion and dill and chop up dill leaves.
5. Mix the salad dressing by adding sour cream, honey, vinegar, and yogurt to a bowl and whisk.
6. By now the cucumber should have released most of its excess water. Tip the bowl to a side and pour the liquid out of the bowl while holding the cucumber slices with your hands. If you leave the water in there, it will water down your dressing and it will eventually become more of a soup than a salad.
7. Add chopped onion and dill to the cucumber, pour dressing over it, give it a good stir and enjoy!

Nutrition Facts
Carbohydrates: 11g Protein: 3g Fat: 4g Saturated Fat: 2g Cholesterol: 11mg Sodium: 617mg Potassium: 332mg Fiber: 1g Sugar: 7g Calcium: 89mg Iron: 1mg

154. Healthy Turkey Lettuce Wraps

Prep Time: 10 Mins
Cook Time: 10 Mins
Total Time: 20 Mins

Ingredients
- 1 pound (454 g) lean ground turkey
- 1 tablespoon (15 ml) vegetable oil
- 1 small onion , diced
- 2 cloves garlic, minced
- 1 teaspoon (5 ml) freshly grated ginger (or 1/2 teaspoon ginger powder)
- 1 bell pepper , diced
- 1 tablespoon (15 ml) soy sauce
- 2 tablespoons (30 ml) hoisin or oyster sauce
- 1 teaspoon (5 ml) sesame oil
- 2 teaspoons (10 ml) rice vinegar or distilled white vinegar (for gluten-free)
- 2 green onions , minced
- Salt , to taste
- Ground black pepper, to taste
- Fresh lettuce leaves

Instructions

1. In a large heated pan, add oil. Add onion, garlic and ginger, and cook until translucent.
2. Add ground turkey and cook for about 3 minutes or until lightly browned. Add soy sauce, hoisin or oyster sauce, sesame oil, rice vinegar and combine with turkey meat.
3. Add bell peppers and green onions and cook for about 5 minutes or until everything is combined well and turkey is cooked through. Add additional salt and pepper to taste.
4. You can serve the filling while it's warm, or allow it to cool. Serve with lettuce leaves.

Nutritional Value
Carbohydrates: 7g, Protein: 28g, Fat: 7g, Saturated Fat: 3g, Cholesterol: 62mg, Sodium: 441mg, Potassium: 458mg, Fiber: 1g, Sugar: 4g, , Calcium: 14mg, Iron: 1.3mg

SNACKS

155. Zucchini Tart With Ricotta And Herbs

Prep Time: 5 Mins
Cook Time: 25 Mins
Total Time: 30 Mins

Ingredients
- 1 roll puff pastry
- 2 zucchini thinly sliced
- 1 cup/250gr fresh ricotta cheese drained
- Handful of basil leaves chopped
- 2 sprigs of fresh thyme chopped
- 1 mozzarella ball drained and chopped (optional)
- Extravirgin olive oil
- Sea salt & black pepper to taste

Instructions
1. Heat oven to 200c/180c fan.
2. Roll out the pastry to about 6 x13inch (15 x 17cm) rectangular shape and trim the edges. Transfer to a baking tray covered with parchment. Score a 1cm border, making sure you don't cut the base.
3. Prick the base with a fork, brush the tart edges of the olive oil. Bake for 15 min, in the oven middle rack.
4. Meanwhile, prepare the cheese filling. In a bowl mix the ricotta, lemon zest, herbs and the mozzarella if using. Drizzle with very little olive oil and season with salt and freshly cracked black pepper.
5. Remove the base from the oven and evenly spread with cheese mixture within the borders.
6. Place zucchini slices along length of the tart.
7. Drizzle with a glug of olive oil, season with sea salt and black pepper and bake for 10 mins more. Remove from the oven and allow to cool slightly. Serve warm or chilled. Refrigerate in an airtight container for up to 2 days. Enjoy!

156. Avocado Goat Cheese Cucumber Appetizers

Prep Time: 15 Minutes
Total Time: 15 Minutes

Ingredients
- 2 ounces fresh goat cheese
- 1 ripe medium avocado
- Dash of tabasco sauce
- 1 tbsp lemon juice
- Pinch of salt
- 1 1/2 medium english cucumbers cut into 1 1/2 inch slices

- 1-2 sundried tomatoes or roasted red peppers chopped finely
- Parsley for garnish

Instructions

1. In a medium-size bowl, with a fork, mash together the avocado and the goat cheese until a smooth mixture is formed. Add a dash of tabasco sauce, lemon juice and salt if desired. Mix until well combined.
2. Slice the cucumber into about 15 slices that are approximately 1 ½ inch in thickness.
3. Spoon or pipe mixture onto cucumber slices and garnish with a small piece of sundried tomato or roasted red pepper and parsley.
4. Nutrition Value
5. Calories: 36kcal Carbohydrates: 2g Protein: 1g Fat: 3g Saturated Fat: 1g Cholesterol: 2mg Sodium: 20mg Potassium: 110mg Fiber: 1g Sugar: 1g Vitamin A: 80iu Vitamin C: 3mg Calcium: 11mg Iron: 1mg

157. Muffins florentine recipe

Total Time: 30 Mins

Ingredients

- 2 cups (15 ounces) unbleached all purpose flour
- 1 tablespoon baking powder
- 1 1/4 teaspoons salt
- 3 large eggs
- 2/3 cups olive oil
- 1 cup milk
- 1 10 ounce package frozen chopped spinach, thawed, drained, and squeezed to remove as much moisture as possible
- 1/2 cup of prepared pesto
- 4 ounces whole milk low moisture mozzarella cheese, shredded

Instructions

1. Preheat the oven to 375 degrees f and spray a 12 cup muffin pan with spray oil.
2. In a large bowl, whisk together the flour, baking powder, and salt.
3. In a medium bowl, whisk the eggs. Whisk in the olive oil, and milk. Stir in the spinach.
4. Add the wet ingredients to the dry ingredients, and stir them in until just combined.
5. Add the pesto and mozzarella and fold until just combined.
6. Scoop the batter into the muffin tin, filling each cavity to the top.
7. Bake the muffins for 20 to 25 minutes, until a toothpick comes out clean.
8. Let the muffins cool in the pan on a wire rack for 5 minutes, remove the muffins from the pan and cool on a wire rack. Serve warm or at room temperature.

158. Spinach Crepes With Pan-Roasted Vegetables

Prep Time: 5 Mins
Cook Time: 25 Mins
Total Time: 30 Mins

Ingredients

Spinach Crepes:

- 1 cup plain flour (140g)
- 4 cups fresh spinach (80g)
- 1 teaspoon pink himalayan salt
- 1 large egg
- 1 thumb-size piece of fresh ginger , grated

- 1 cup milk (250ml)
- 1 tablespoon dried oregano
- 1 cup grated cheese of your choice
- Sunflower oil for frying

Pan-Roasted Vegetables:
- 2 cups chopped mushrooms (120g)
- 1 yellow bell pepper
- 1 medium onion
- 2 cups cherry tomatoes (280g)
- 2 cups chopped flat leaf parsley (100g)
- 1 cup grated cheese of your choice
- 3 garlic cloves
- 3 tablespoons butter (45g)
- ½ teaspoon pink himalayan salt

Instructions
1. In a food processor/blender process spinach & milk until smooth. Pour this in a mixing bowl. Add flour, salt, egg and grated ginger. Whisk until well combined.
2. Heat up your frying pan. Add a tiny amount of oil and pour the batter in – use a ¼ measuring cup. Spread around evenly by lifting the pan and turning it allowing the batter spread.
3. Once set, turn it over and cook for a further 1/2 minute to a minute (or until cooked).

Pan-Roasted Vegetables:
1. In a frying pan, melt butter. Add sliced onion, mushrooms and pepper (cut into strips). Roast for 10 minutes before adding cherry tomatoes & garlic. Roast for a further 2-3 minutes. Turn off the heat and stir in parsley.
2. Top or fill pancakes with vegetable mixture and sprinkle with grated cheese.
3. Best served while still warm!

Nutrition Facts
Fat: 18g Saturated Fat: 8g Cholesterol: 56mg Sodium: 907mg Potassium: 579mg Carbohydrates: 24g Fiber: 3g Sugar: 4g Protein: 15g

159. Kale Kefir Pancakes

Prep Time: 10 Mins
Cook Time: 6 Mins
Total Time: 16 Mins

Ingredients
- 300 ml kefir, buttermilk or sour milk
- Large handful of kale (about 75g) – washed with excess water shaken off
- 100 g rolled oats make sure they're gluten-free if necessary
- Pinch sea salt
- 1 large egg (i used a duck egg)
- 150 g buckwheat flour or a good gluten-free flour mix
- 1 tsp baking powder
- ¼ tsp bicarbonate of soda
- 1 tsp turmeric
- Good grinding of black pepper
- 1 tbsp coconut oil for frying

Instructions
1. Blitz the kale, oats and salt with the kefir in a power blender until you have a smoothish and bright green batter. I used my optimum g2.3 for 90 seconds.
2. Add all the other ingredients except for the coconut oil and blitz for a further 20 seconds or until everything is well mixed.
3. Place a non-stick frying pan on a medium heat and add a little of the coconut oil.
4. Pour dollops of batter into the pan, making sure there is room for them to spread. How many you get in will depend on how big the pan is.

5. Cook for about 3 minutes or until bubbles start to rise up in the batter, then flip over and fry for a further 3 minutes.
6. Stack on a plate and put in a warm oven until all of the pancakes are cooked.

Nutrition Value
Calories: 325kcal Carbohydrates: 48.8g Protein: 11.7g
Fat: 9.8g   Saturated Fat: 5.4g   Cholesterol: 56mg
Sodium: 206mg Potassium: 339mg Fiber: 7.9g Sugar: 4.7g Calcium: 80mg Iron: 2mg

160. Okonomiyaki

Prep Time: 15 Minutes
Cook Time: 15 Minutes
Total Time: 30 Minutes

Ingredients
- 1 tbsp ground flaxseeds
- 3 tbsp water
- Sunflower oil for frying
- 4 medium shiitake or chestnut mushrooms, finely chopped
- 50g buckwheat flour
- 50g rice flour
- ¼ tsp salt
- 200ml dashi stock or water
- 150g white cabbage, thinly shredded
- 3 spring onions, finely sliced and 1 tbsp reserved for garnish
- 1 sheet sushi nori, snipped into small thin strips with scissors, 1 tbsp reserved for garnish

Topping
- 2-3 tbsp vegan mayonnaise
- Japanese 'bull dog sauce'
- 2 tsp seaweed flakes
- 1 tbsp pickled ginger, shredded thinly
- 1 tbsp sliced pickled lotus root
- Togarashi chilli seasoning

Instructions
1. Mix the ground flaxseeds with the 3 tablespoons water and allow to stand for 10 minutes.
2. Heat 1 tablespoon of sunflower oil in a frying pan on a medium to high heat, and quickly stir fry the mushrooms till golden and just becoming slightly crisp. Set aside to cool.
3. Mix the flours, salt, soaked ground flaxseed mixture and water or dashi stock together to make a batter. Add the fried mushrooms, shredded cabbage, spring onions, nori strips and mix well to combine. You may to need to add a tablespoon or two more water if the mixture feels too thick but it needs to be just thick enough to hold the vegetables together.
4. Heat 1 tablespoon of sunflower oil in a frying pan over a medium heat, then spoon half the mixture into the centre of the pan. Use a spoon to spread the mixture into a round pancake about 15cm diameter and 3cm thick. Place a lid on the pan to cover and cook the pancake for 3 minutes, checking occasionally for the base to get a good golden brown colour.
5. Remove the lid and carefully flip the pancake over, then cover again and cook for another 3 minutes, till it feels firm in the centre when pressed. Slide carefully onto a serving plate.
6. Repeat with the remaining mixture to make a second pancake.
7. Serve hot with bull dog sauce spread over the top and mayonnaise drizzled over in a zigzag pattern. Scatter the reserved spring onions over, a pinch of nori strips, a teaspoon of seaweed flakes, some thinly shredded pickled ginger, pickled lotus root and a sprinkle of togarashi chilli seasoning.

Nutrition Facts
Total Fat: 3.3g Saturated Fat:0.9g Polyunsaturated Fat:0.7g   Cholesterol:106.2mg   Sodium:37.0mg Potassium:151.4mg Carbohydrate 61.2g Dietary Fiber 2.5g Protein: 11.5g.

161. Holy Guacamole Recipe

Prep Time: 10 Minutes
Cook Time: 0 Minutes
Total Time: 10 Minutes
Servings: 8

Ingredients
- 3 large ripe Haas avocados
- 1 lime, juiced
- 2-3 cloves garlic, minced
- 1 jalapeno, minced
- 1/4 cup green onions, chopped
- 1/4 cup cilantro, chopped
- 1 plum tomatoes, diced
- Salt and pepper, to taste

Instructions
1. Cut the avocados in half, remove the pit, and scoop the flesh out with a spoon. Place the avocado flesh in a medium bowl and pour the lime juice over the top. Use a spoon and fork to mash the avocado until mostly smooth.
2. Smell your jalapeño to test the heat... You can usually tell if you got a spicy one. Stir in the garlic, jalapeño (half or all), green onions, and cilantro. Salt and pepper to taste. Stir in the diced tomato at the very end.
3. Serve immediately, or press plastic wrap down over the surface of the guacamole, removing all air bubbles, and refrigerate until ready to serve.

Nutrition
Calories: 127kcal, Carbohydrates: 8g, Protein: 1g, Fat: 11g, Saturated Fat: 1g, Cholesterol: 0mg, Sodium: 6mg, Potassium: 401mg, Fiber: 5g, Sugar: 0g, Vitamin A: 260iu, Vitamin C: 14.1mg, Calcium: 15mg, Iron: 0.5mg

162. Crispy Kohlrabi Slaw

Prep Time: 25 Minutes
Cook Time: 0 Minutes
Total Time: 25 Minutes
Servings: 8 Serving

Ingredients
- 4 C kohlrabi, sliced into matchsticks
- 1/4 C cilantro, chopped
- 1 teaspoons Phoenix Sunrise Seasoning (or your favorite no-salt taco-style seasoning)
- 1 teaspoons Kickin' Cajun Seasoning* (or garlic, salt, black pepper, cumin, cayenne pepper, and onion)
- Zest of 1 lime
- Zest of 1 orange
- juice of 1 lime
- 4 teaspoons Valencia Orange Oil (or your favorite oil and fresh-squeezed orange juice)

Instructions
1. Place all ingredients, except the kohlrabi & cilantro into a large salad bowl. Whisk to combine.
2. Add the kohlrabi to the bowl, sprinkle with cilantro.
3. Using two large spoons, pull the dressing up through the salad by placing the spoons at the bottom of the bowl and scooping the kohlrabi mixture upward. Keep tossing until fully coated.
4. Set aside for 15 minutes up to a day ahead of time and serve chilled.

Nutrition
Calories: 38 Total Fat: 2.3g Sat Fat: 0.3g Cholesterol: 0mg Sodium: 14mg Carbohydrates: 4.2g Fiber: 2.5g Sugar: 1.8g Protein: 1.2g Calcium: 17mg Iron: 0mg Potassium: 237mg

163. Lemon Dill Roasted Radishes

Prep Time: 5 Minutes
Cook Time: 30 Minutes
Total Time: 35 Minutes
Servings: 4 Serving

Ingredients
- 4 C red radish halves, greens, and stems removed
- 2 teaspoons high quality cooking oil of your choice
- 1/2 T Citrus Dill Seasoning
- 1/2 T Brightening Blend (or freshly squeezed lemon)

Instructions
1. preheat oven to 350 degrees
2. Trim ends and tops of radishes, cut in half (all radish pieces should be about the same size- if you have small ones, leave them whole, big ones should be cut in 1/4, etc)
3. Add all ingredients to a large bowl and toss to coat.
4. Place radishes in an oven-safe roasting dish and place in oven, center rack, for 30 minutes. If you have a cast-iron skillet, this is the PERFECT time to use it!
5. Serve hot

Nutrition
- Calories: 39 Total Fat: 2.4g Sat Fat: 0.3g Cholesterol: 0mg Sodium: 45mg Carbohydrates: 3.9g Fiber: 1.9g Sugar: 2.2g Protein: 0.8g Calcium: 29mg Iron: 0mg Potassium: 270mg

164. Low Carb Sloppy Joes

Prep Time: 5 Minutes
Cook Time: 25 Minutes
Total Time: 30 Minutes

Ingredients
- 1 1/2 pounds lean ground beef
- 1/2 C diced green bell pepper
- 2 Tablespoons tomato paste
- 1 teaspoon (one packet) powdered stevia
- 1 Tablespoon yellow mustard
- 1Tablespoon of salt, pepper, crushed garlic, garlic powder, and onion to taste
- 1/2 Tablespoon
- 1Tablespoon red wine vinegar
- 1 C low sodium beef broth
- Salt and Pepper to taste

Instructions
1. Place the ground beef in a frying pan and place on the stove over medium heat. Break up the larger pieces of meat as it is cooking.
2. Let the meat cook for about 7 minutes and then add the remaining ingredients (EXCEPT the broth) and stir to combine. Once mixed, add the water and turn up the heat to medium-high.
3. Once the liquid is boiling, reduce the heat to low and let it simmer, uncovered for about 10-15 minutes until the liquid is somewhat reduced & you have a lovely sauce.
4. Serve hot & enjoy!

Nutrition
Calories: 302 Total Fat: 11.5g Sat Fat: 5.2g Cholesterol: 132mg Sodium: 189mg Carbohydrates: 2.7g Fiber: 0.6g

Sugar: 1g Protein: 44.1g Calcium: 25g Iron: 5mg Potassium: 776mg

165. Fresh Lime Crema

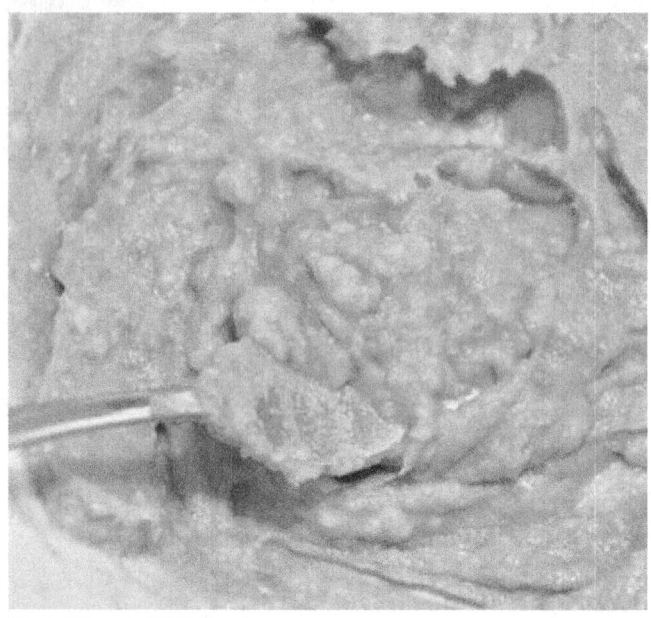

Prep Time: 10 Minutes
Cook Time: 0 Minutes
Total Time: 10 Minutes
Servings: 4+ Serving

Ingredients
- 1 Cup sour cream
- 1teaspoon salt, pepper, garlic, and onion to taste
- Zest from one lime
- Juice from one lime
- 1/4 C fresh cilantro, finely shredded if desired

Instructions
1. Place all ingredients in a mixing bowl and stir vigorously to combine.
2. Let rest for 15 minutes before serving to allow flavors to develop. May be stored in an airtight container, refrigerated for up to one week.

Nutrition
Calories: 27 Total Fat: 2.5g Sat Fat: 1.6g Cholesterol: 5mg Sodium: 7mg Carbohydrates: 1g Fiber: 0.1g Sugar: 0.1g Protein: 0.4g Calcium: 15g Iron: 0mg Potassium: 24mg

166. Fresh Pico De Gallo

Prep Time: 15 Minutes
Cook Time: 0 Minutes
Total Time: 15 Minutes
Servings: 2+ Serving

Ingredients
- 1 C diced tomatoes (fresh or canned and well-drained)
- 1/4 C (4 Tablespoons) fresh onion, finely chopped
- 1teaspoon of salt, pepper, garlic, and onion to taste
- 2 T finely chopped cilantro
- Juice of one fresh lime

Instructions
1. Place all ingredients in a bowl and toss gently to combine.
2. For best flavor, let sit for 15 minutes before serving.

Nutrition
Calories: 20 Total Fat: 0.2g Sat Fat: 0g Cholesterol: 0mg Sodium: 7mg Carbohydrates: 4.6g Fiber: 1.2g Sugar: 2.6g Protein: 0.8g Calcium: 11g Iron: 0mg Potassium: 225mg

167. Tex-Mex Seared Salmon

Prep Time: 5 Minutes
Cook Time: 15 Minutes
Total Time: 20 Minutes
Servings: 4 Serving

Ingredients
- 1 1/2 pounds wild-caught salmon filet (will cook best if you have it at room temp)
- 1 Tablespoon (one Capful) of salt, pepper, garlic, cumin, paprika, cayenne, and onion to taste

Instructions
1. Preheat a nonstick pan over high heat for 1 minute.
2. While heating, sprinkle seasoning over the salmon (NOT on the skin side)
3. Reduce heat to medium-high.
4. Place the fish, seasoning side down in the pan and let it cook for 4-6 minutes depending on thickness. You'll know it's ready to flip when a "crust" has formed from the seasoning and the fish releases from the pan easily.
5. Reduce heat to medium-low. Flip the fish over to the skin side down and cook an additional 4-6 minutes.
6. Remove from heat and serve. Fish should slide right off the skin and onto the plate. The serving size is 5 ounces of salmon

Nutrition
Calories: 192 Total Fat: 8.8g Sat Fat: 1.3g Cholesterol: 63mg Sodium: 147mg Carbohydrates: 0.8g Fiber: 0g Sugar: 0.2g Protein: 22.5g Calcium: 50mg Iron: 1mg Potassium: 544mg

FUELING HACKS RECIPES

168. Spring Green Smoothie Breakfast Drink

Prep Time: 20 Minutes
Total Time: 20 Minutes

Ingredients
- 1 cup buttermilk
- 1 cup plain kefir
- 1 banana
- 3 cups frozen fruit, i used mango, strawberry, pineapple frozen blend
- 1 cup dandelion greens-chopped
- 3 cups kale greens-chopped
- 2 tablespoons maple syrup, to taste

Instructions
1. Pour the kefir and buttermilk into your blender.
2. Add the chopped greens 1/3 at a time and pulse a few times until blended.
3. Add banana and pulse twice
4. Add frozen fruit and blend until thoroughly mixed.
5. 2 tablespoons maple syrup(or honey) to taste

Nutritional Facts
Fat: 3.5g Sat Fat: 1.8g Cholesterol: 10mg Sodium: 129mg Carbohydrate: 44.7g Fiber: 5.2g Sugar: 32.5g Protein: 7.5g

169. Nectarine And Avocado Smoothie

Prep Time: 5 Mins
Total Time: 5 Mins
Ingredients
For The Nectarine Layer:
- 3 nectarines chopped
- ½ mango peeled and chopped
- 150 ml unsweetened coconut water

For The Avocado Layer:
- 1 large avocado chopped
- A handful of fresh baby spinach leaves
- 1 tsp wholesome organic stevia
- 150 ml unsweetened coconut water

Instructions
1. Start with the green layer of the smoothie. In a powerful blender, (such as vitamix) place chopped avocado, spinach, wholesome organic stevia and coconut water. Blend until smooth and divide between two glasses.
2. Rinse the blender, and fold in chopped nectarines, mango and coconut water. Blend until smooth and pour over the green smoothie.
3. Serve immediately.

Nutritional Value
Calories: 319kcal Carbohydrates: 45g Protein: 6g Fat: 16g Saturated Fat: 3g Sodium: 181mg Potassium: 1489mg Fiber: 13g Sugar: 29g

170. Morning Green Juice

Prep Time: 5 Mins
Total Time: 5 Mins
Ingredients
- 2 celery stalks
- ½ cucumber ends cut off
- 1 green apple cored
- ½ tsp grated ginger
- A bunch of fresh spinach leaves
- 6 fresh mint leaves

Instructions
1. **Green Juice In A Juicer Recipe:** Place the celery stalks into the juicer and juice. Repeat with the other ingredients in the order listed until all ingredients are juiced. Pour into a glass and serve.
2. **Green Juice In A Blender Recipe:** Put celery, cucumber, apple, ginger and half a glass of water into your blender, then pulse until liquefied. Add the spinach and mint leaves and pulse until liquefied. Pour into a glass and serve.

Nutritional Facts
Carbohydrates: 29g Protein: 16g Fat: 16g Calcium: 148mg Iron: 2mg

171. Peanut Butter Green Smoothie

Prep Time: 5 Minutes
Total Time: 5 Minutes
Ingredients
- ½ cup unsweetened non-dairy milk, (i used organic soy)
- 2 medjool dates, pits removed
- 1 cup kale, ribs removed, roughly chopped (or substitute fresh spinach)
- 1 tablespoon peanut butter, (or other nut butter)
- 1 frozen banana

Instructions
1. Add the non-dairy milk, dates, and chopped kale to your high-speed blender. Place the lid on and blend until the greens are partially broken down.
2. Next add the peanut butter and frozen banana. Place the lid on and blend again until completely smooth, using the tamper, as needed. (the tamper is the stick that comes with your blender that assists with pushing ingredients toward the blade.)
3. Pour in a glass and enjoy right away.

Nutrition
Calories: 418kcal   Carbohydrates: 76g   Protein: 13g   Fat: 11g   Saturated Fat: 2g   Sodium: 160mg   Potassium: 1356mg   Fiber: 8g   Sugar: 51g   Vitamin A: 7304iu   Vitamin C: 99mg   Calcium: 296mg   Iron: 3mg

172. Pistachio Muffins

Prep Time: 5 Mins
Cook Time: 15 Mins
Total Time: 20 Mins
Ingredients
- 140 g butter softened
- 140 g muscovado sugar
- 2 large eggs beaten
- 140 g self-raising flour
- Zest of 1 orange
- 1 tbsp matcha green tea
- 1 tsp baking powder
- 1 very ripe banana mashed
- 4 tbsp pistachio chopped plus extra for decorating

Instructions
1. Cream the butter and sugar until light and fluffy, then slowly add the eggs with a little flour.
2. Fold in the remaining flour, banana, matcha tea, pistachio, orange zest, a pinch of salt and baking powder.
3. Pour the mixture into a prepared muffin tin, filling almost to the top each mould. Top each muffin with extra chopped pistachio and a pinch of caster sugar.
4. Bake for about 5 mins at 425f/200c, then lower to 360f/180c and continue to bake for 10 mins, or until a skewer comes out clean.
5. Cool in the tin for 10 mins, then remove to a wire rack and serve. Enjoy!

Nutrition Facts
Calories: 241kcal   Carbohydrates: 33g   Protein: 6g   Fat: 11g   Saturated Fat: 1g   Sodium: 6mg   Potassium:

313mg Fiber: 13g Sugar: 15g Vitamin A: 95iu Calcium: 243mg Iron: 3mg

173. Skillet Mexican Zucchini

Prep Time: 5 Mins
Cook Time: 10 Mins
Total Time: 15 Mins

Ingredients
- 1 garlic clove, finely chopped
- 1 tbsp extra virgin olive oil
- 1 lb zucchini, diced
- 1 large tomato, cored, seeded and diced
- 1 green onion, thinly sliced
- 1 tbsp minced fresh cilantro
- 1 tsp minced pickled jalapeño
- 1/2 cup crumbled queso blanco, or queso fresco, cotija or feta
- Fresh lime juice, to taste
- Salt, to taste
- Freshly ground black pepper, to taste

Instructions
1. Cook the garlic in oil in a large skillet over medium heat 1 minute, stirring until sizzling.
2. Add zucchini and cook stirring occasionally, about 3 minutes or until slightly softened.
3. Add the tomato and green onion and cook about 3 minutes.
4. Remove skillet from heat and add cilantro, jalapeño and lime juice.
5. Season with salt and pepper to taste and top with queso blanco. Serve hot.

Nutritional Value

Carbohydrates: 8g Protein: 5g Fat: 6g Cholesterol: 17mg Sodium: 211mg Fiber: 2g Sugar: 3g

174. Coconut Green Smoothie

Prep Time: 5 Minutes

Ingredients:
- 1 sachet Green Renewal Shake
- 1 small Ice (optional)*
- 1 stalk Celery chopped
- 1 cup Raw Baby Spinach (optional)*
- 1 stalk Kale (optional)*
- 1 tbsp Fresh Mint
- 1 tbsp Hemp Seeds
- 1/2 cup Cucumber chopped
- 1/2 cup Refrigerated Unsweetened Coconut Milk

Instructions:
1. Place all ingredients in blender, and blend on high for 1 or 2 minutes or until desired consistency is reached

175. Tiramisu Shake

Prep Time: 5 Minutes
Ingredients:
- 1 sachet Frosty Coffee Soft Serve Treat
- 1/2 cup Ice
- 6 oz Plain Non-Fat Greek Yogurt
- 1/2 cup Unsweetened Almond Milk (optional)*
- 1/2 cup Cashew Milk (optional)*
- 2 tbsp Sugar-free Chocolate Syrup
- 2 tbsp Pressurized Whipped Topping

Instructions
1. Combine all the ingredients in a blender, and blend until smooth.
2. Pour into a glass or mason jar. Drizzle with syrup, and top with whipped topping.

176. Cumin and Cheese Hack

Prep Time: 4 Minutes
Ingredients:
- 1 sachet Sour Cream & Chives Smashed Potatoes
- 1/8 tsp Cayenne Pepper
- 1 tsp Cumin
- 1 tbsp Reduced-Fat Cheddar Cheese shredded
- 2 tsp Cholula Hot Sauce

Instructions
1. Prepare Sour Cream & Chives Smashed Potatoes as per package.
2. Add cumin and cayenne pepper and mix thoroughly.
3. Top with reduced-fat cheddar cheese and cholula
4. Enjoy
5.

177. Cauliflower Wings

Prep Time: 5 Minutes
Cooking Time: 25 Minutes
Total Time: 30 Minutes

Ingredients:
- 2 sachet Buttermilk Cheddar Herb Biscuit
- 1/2 cup Water
- 3 cup Cauliflower Florets
- 1 can Cooking spray
- 1/4 cup Hot Buffalo Sauce
- 1/2 tbsp Unsalted Butter melted
- 1/4 cup Low-fat Greek Yogurt
- 1 tsp Dry Ranch Dressing Mix

Instructions
1. Preheat oven to 425*F.
2. In a medium-sized bowl, mix buttermilk cheddar herb biscuits and water. Add cauliflower florets, and toss until evenly coated in batter.
3. Place cauliflower florets onto a lightly greased foil-lined baking sheet. Bake for 20 minutes.
4. In another bowl combine the hot sauce and butter. Add the baked cauliflower and toss to coat the florets. Place back on the baking sheet and bake for another 7 to 10 minutes.
5. In a small bowl, combine yogurt and ranch mix. Serve the cauliflower wings with the ranch dip.

178. Neapolitan Popsicles

Prep Time: 25 Minutes

Ingredients:
- 1 cup Unsweetened Vanilla Almond Milk divided (optional)*
- 1 cup Cashew Milk divided (optional)*
- 2 cup Low-fat Greek Yogurt divided
- 1 sachet Essentials Creamy Chocolate Shake
- 1 sachet Essential Creamy Vanilla Shake
- 1 sachet Essential Wild Strawberry Shake
- 1 packet Zero-calorie sugar substitute

Instructions
1. Add 1/3 cup (choose either unsweetened vanilla almond OR cashew) milk, 2/3 cup plain Greek yogurt, Creamy Chocolate Shake, and 1/3 of a packet of sugar substitute to a blender; blend until smooth.
2. Distribute mixture evenly among the bottoms of 6 large popsicle mold, and place in the freezer for 15 minutes (to help set the popsicles a bit).
3. Repeat steps 1 & 2 with the Creamy Vanilla Shake (15 minutes freeze again), and then the Wild Strawberry Shake.
4. After repeating all the steps freeze until set, at least 4 hours or overnight.

179. Mint Chocolate Muffins

Prep Time: 10 Minutes
Ingredients:
- 4 sachet Essential Chocolate Mint Cookie Crisp Bars
- 12 oz Low-fat Greek Yogurt
- 2 tbsp Sugar-free Chocolate Pudding Mix

1/4 tsp Peppermint Extract

Instructions
1. Line a standard-sized muffin tin with eight cupcakes liners.
2. Break each Chocolate Mint Cookie Crisp Bar in half. Place bar halves crunch-side down on a microwave-safe plate, and microwave for 20 to 30 seconds, until softened.
3. Place each half into the bottom of a cupcake liner, and press down to form a thin crust. Repeat until all cupcake liners are filled.
4. In a large bowl, mix low-fat plain Greek yogurt and sugar-free, fat-free chocolate pudding mix until well combined.
5. Evenly distribute yogurt and pudding mixture among cupcake liners.
6. Freeze for 30 to 60 minutes, until solid. Garnish tops with fresh mint leaves if desired, and serve immediately.

180. Zucchini Bread

Ingredients:
- Any Pancake packet
- 1/4 c. shredded zucchini (squeeze out the liquid by rolling in paper towels and squeezing) (1/2 of 1 Green)
- 2 tbsp egg beaters
- oz water
- 1 packet Stevia

Directions:
1. Mix together and bake in whatever style you'd like.
2. I did it on the waffle iron, super fast and yummy zucchini bread waffle.
3. I think I'll try mini muffins next, or even as just a pancake.
4. If you decide to bake these, bake at 350 degrees.
5. The time will vary depending on what type of pan you are using.

181. Oatmeal Cookies

Ingredients:
- 1 pkt. Medifast or Lean & Green oatmeal (1 Fueling)
- 1 Medifast or Lean & Green oatmeal raisin crunch bar (1 Fueling)
- 1/8 tsp cinnamon (1/4 Condiment)
- 1 pkt Stevia ~ optional
- 1/3 cup water
- 1/8 tsp baking powder (1/4 Condiment)
- 1/2 tsp vanilla
- 2 tbsp PB2 - Optional (1 Optional Snack)

Directions:
1. Preheat oven to 350 degrees.
2. Microwave oatmeal raisin bar for about 15 sec until slightly melted.
3. Mix the bar with all the other ingredients and let sit for 5 minutes.
4. Line a cookie sheet with parchment paper or spray with cooking spray.
5. Drop by spoonfuls to make 4 cookies. Bake for 12-15 minutes.

182. Mint Cookies

Prep Time: 5 Mins
Total Time: 15 Mins

Ingredients
- 2 sachet Lean & Green Essential Decadent Double Chocolate Brownie
- 2 bar Lean & Green Essential Chocolate Mint Cookie Crisp Bars
- 1 tbsp Liquid Egg Substitute
- 2 tbsp Unsweetened Almond Milk (optional)*
- 2 tbsp Cashew Milk (optional)*
- 1/4 tsp Mint Extract

Instructions:
1. Preheat oven to 350*F.
2. Microwave Chocolate Mint Cookie Crisp Bars for 15 to 20 seconds, until softened.
3. In a small bowl, combine Decadent Double Chocolate Brownies, liquid egg substitute, milk (unsweetened almond OR cashew) milk, and mint extract. Stir in microwave crunch bars (will break apart into tiny pieces).
4. Form mixture into eight, cookie-shaped pieces onto a parchment-lined baking sheet.
5. Bake for 12 to 15 minutes, until firm.

183. Shrimp Salad

Prep Time: 5 Mins
Total Time: 10 Mins
Ingredients
- 2 lbs Raw Shrimp
- 1 lbs fresh whole Tomatoes
- 1 small Jalapeno Peppers finely chopped
- 1 small Garlic Cloves
- 2 stalk Scallions
- 1/2 tbsp Olive Oil
- 1 tsp Dried Oregano
- 8 medium Green Olives halved
- 4 tbsp Lime Juice
- 1/2 cup Fresh Cilantro chopped
- 1 medium Avocado diced
- 2 1/2 cup Romaine Lettuce
- 1/4 tsp Salt (optional)*
- 1/4 tsp Black Pepper

Instructions:
Preheat oven to broil.
1. Bring a medium size pot of water to a boil and cook shrimp about 2 to 3 minutes until pink.
2. Remove shrimp and shock in an ice bath until cooked
3. Drain, pat dry, and set aside.
4. Toss tomatoes, jalapeno, garlic, and scallions in olive oil.
5. Transfer to a sheet pan and broil about 5 to 10 minutes until outside skin is charred.
6. Remove pan and allow to cool long enough to handle.
7. Remove core from tomatoes, stem from jalapeno, skin from garlic, and root of scallions.
8. Place in a food processor and pulse until chopped or desired consistency.
9. Transfer tomato mixture to a mixing bowl.
10. Add olives, lime juice, cilantro, avocado, shrimp, and toss well. Season with salt (optional) and pepper to taste.
11. Pour over lettuce and serve.

184. Peanut Butter Cookies

Prep Time: 10 Mins
Total Time: 12 Mins
Ingredients
- 4 sachet Essential Silky Peanut Butter Shake
- 1/4 tsp Baking Powder
- 1/4 tsp Unsweeted Original (optional)*
- 1 tbsp Butter (optional)*
- 1/4 tsp Vanilla Extract
- 1 can Light Cooking Spray
- 1/8 tsp Sea Salt (optional)*

Instructions:
1. Preheat oven to 350*F. Line a baking sheet with foil and spray with cooking spray.
2. In a medium-sized bowl, mix together the first two ingredients.
3. Add the milk (1/4 cup unsweetened original, vanilla almond or cashew milk), butter or (margarine, melted or softened), and vanilla extract, stir until well combined (it will appear dry, but continue mixing until a dough forms - add another tablespoon of milk if necessary)
4. Using a small cookie scoop, scoop out dough into 8 small balls, and place onto the foil-lined, lightly greased baking sheet.

5. Using a fork, flatten the mounds to create a criss-cross pattern.
6. Bake until edges are lightly browned, approximately 10 to 12 minutes. Serve with unsweetened original, or vanilla almond milk if desired

185. Pumpkin Pie Frappe

Prep Time: 5 Mins
Ingredients
- 1 sachet Essentials Spiced Gingerbread
- 4 oz Unsweetened Vanilla Almond Milk
- 4 oz Strong Brewed Coffee
- 1/2 cup Ice
- 1/8 tsp Pumpkin Pie Spice
- 2 tbsp Pressurized Whipped Topping

Instructions:
1. Combine 1sachet Spiced Gingerbread, 4oz. milk your choice, 4oz. strong brewed coffee (chilled), 1/2 cup ice, and 1/8 to 1/4 tsp. pumpkin pie spice depending on how strong of pumpkin taste you desire.
2. Blend in a blender until smooth.
3. Top with whipped topping, and serve. Enjoy!

186. Peanut Butter Brownie

Prep Time: 5 Mins
Total Time: 20 Mins
Ingredients
- 2 sachet Essential Double Chocolate Brownie
- 1/4 tsp Baking Powder
- 3 tbsp Egg Whites
- 6 tbsp Unsweetened Almond Milk
- 1 tsp Vegetable Oil
- 1/4 cup Powdered Peanut Butter
- 2 dash Light Cooking Spray

Instructions:
1. Preheat oven to 350° F
2. In a medium-sized bowl, combine Lean & Green Double Chocolate Brownie mixture, baking powder, egg substitute, almond milk, and oil, and mix until a batter-like consistency.
3. Divide batter evenly among 4 slots of a lightly-greased muffin tin (should fill only a third of each slot). Bake until a toothpick inserted in center comes out clean, about 18 to 20 minutes.
4. Meanwhile, combine powdered peanut butter and remaining milk.
5. Once cooled, slice each muffin in half horizontally. Spread one tablespoon of peanut butter filling onto the bottom half of each muffin, and top with the remaining muffin halves

187. Pancake Cinnamon Buns

Prep Time: 10 Mins
Ingredients:
- 1 MF Pancake Mix
- 1 packet Stevia
- 1/8 tsp Baking Powder
- 1/4 tsp Cinnamon
- 2 tbsp water
- 1/4 tsp Vanilla Extract)
- 5 Sprays I Can't Believe It's Not Butter Spray (1/2 Healthy Fat)

Directions:
1. Put all ingredients in a small bowl except ICBNB spray. Mix gently.
2. Try not to work the batter too much.
3. Spray a small microwavable bowl or mug with Pam. One of the Medifast Brownie dishes is good for this, too. Spoon the batter into the bowl/mug/dish, and dust the top with cinnamon.
4. Microwave for 40 seconds. Pull out and spray the top with ICBINB spray. Eat and enjoy!

188. Cinnamon Roll

Prep Time: 15 Mins
Ingredients:
- 1 pancake mix
- 2 tbsp water
- 1/8 tsp cinnamon
- 1 tbsp light cream cheese)
- 1 packet Stevia, divided
- Few sprays of I Can't Believe It's Not Butter Spray

Directions:
1. Combine pancake mix, cinnamon, half packet of Stevia, and water.
2. Pour into a small container.
3. Microwave for 50 seconds.
4. Make sure you do not overcook it otherwise it will get dry.
5. Spray the pancake with ICBINB spray.
6. In the same bowl you used to make the pancake batter, combine cream cheese and the rest of the splenda.
7. Mix around with the little bit of batter that was left in the bowl.
8. This adds a bit of the cinnamon mixture into the cream cheese.
9. Spread on pancake.

189. Pumpkin Pie Custard

Prep Time: 10 Mins

Ingredients:
- 1 package of Vanilla pudding
- 1 egg white
- 1/2 tsp vanilla extract
- 1/2 tsp pumpkin pie spice
- 1 packet Stevia
- 1/2 cup water

Directions:
1. Preheat oven to 350 degrees.
2. Spray a ramekin with cooking spray. Mix all ingredients in a blender.
3. Pour into prepared ramekin. Bake for 20 to 25 minutes or until set.
4. Serve warm or refrigerate overnight.
5. I put mine in the fridge overnight.

190. Chocolate Cookies

Prep Time 20 Minutes

Ingredients:
- 1 Brownie Mix
- 1 Peanut Butter Chocolate Crunch Bar or crunch bar of your choice
- 3 tbsp water

Directions:
1. Combine brownie mix with 3 tbsp water and set aside.
2. Place the crunch bar on a dish in the microwave for 20 seconds on high until it is slightly melted.
3. Add the crunch bar into the brownie mixture until blended.
4. Place the mixture into two separate ramekins or on a plate sprayed lightly with cooking spray.
5. Microwave for 2 minutes.
6. Let cool for 5 min.

191. Brownie Ice Cream

Prep Time 25 Minutes
Ingredients:
- 1 Brownie Mix
- 1 Peanut Butter Crunch Bar
- 3 tbsp water
- 2 tbsp PB2 (1 Snack)
- 1 tbsp water
- 2 tbsp cool whip

Directions:
1. Melt 1 brownie and 1 peanut butter crunch for 20 seconds.
2. Add 3 tbsp water and mix. Spray a plate with cooking spray.
3. Drop 4 spoonfuls of dough on plate. Microwave for 2 minutes.
4. Mix PB2 and water to firm a paste.
5. Add peanut butter mixture to each of two cookies and then add 1 tbsp of cool whip to each of the other two cookies.
6. Place peanut butter cookie on top of cookie with whip cream.
7. Place stuffed cookies in Ziploc container and freeze thoroughly.
8. Each cookie is one meal.

192. Chocolate Coffee Muffins

Prep Time 20 Minutes
Ingredients:
- 1 packet MF Cappuccino
- 1 packet MF Chocolate Chip
- 1 packet of Stevia
- 1 tbsp Egg Beaters
- 1/4 tsp baking powder
- 1/4 cup Water

Cream Cheese Frosting
- 2 tbsp light cream cheese - Optional (2 Condiments)
- 1/2 packet Stevia - Optional (1/2 Condiment)

Directions:
1. Mix ingredients together.
2. Pour into a 4 inch round or square plastic microwavable dish that has been sprayed with Pam.
3. Microwave on high for 1 min. 45 sec - 2 min, checking for consistency.
4. Eat immediately.

193. Pancake Muffins

Prep Time 15 Minutes
Ingredients:
- 1 Pancake mix
- 1/4 cup water

Directions:
1. Combine pancake mix and water in a shaker jar.
2. Shake well until combined.
3. Pour mixture into a glass mug sprayed with Pam that is the same shape all around.
4. Or pour into a small square container for bread. Microwave for 1 1/2 minutes.
5. Pour out of glass or container and slice

194. Pecan Ice Cream

Prep Time 20 Minutes
Ingredients:
- Vanilla Pudding
- 1/2 cup ice cubes, crushed
- 3 oz water
- 1/4 tsp coconut extract
- 1/4 tsp almond extract
- 1/2 tsp maple extract
- 1 tbsp Walden Farms caramel syrup - optional

Directions:
1. Put all ingredients into blender.
2. Mix ingredients for 2 to 3 minutes until smooth.

| 195. Chocolate Peanut Cup | 196. Peanut Brownie and Greek Yogurt |

Prep Time 10 Minutes

Ingredients:
- 1 package Hot Cocoa or brownie mix
- 2 tablespoon PB2
- 1 packet of Stevia

Directions:
1. Mix 2 tablespoon of PB2 and stevia with 1 1/2 tablespoon of water
2. Set aside. In another container, mix hot cocoa with 3 tablespoons of water.
3. Spread half over the bottom of a ramekin or silicone baking cup.
4. Spread PB2 over the chocolate bottom layer.
5. Spread the rest of the hot cocoa mixture over the top of the PB2.
6. Place in freezer for at least one hour.

Prep Time: 5 Minutes

Ingredients:
- 1 packet Medifast/ Lean & Green Brownie
- 5.3 oz container of low fat plain Greek yogurt
- 1 tbsp PB2 or PBFit

Directions:
1. Combine the three ingredients in a medium sized bowl and stir until combined.
2. Mixture will be thick.
3. Enjoy!

197. Cheese Tomato Sandwich

Prep Time: 15 Minutes
Ingredients:
- 1 packet Medifast Cream of Tomato Soup
- 1/4 cup egg beaters
- 1 slice 2% Reduced Fat American cheese

Directions:
1. Mix soup and egg beaters together.
2. Pour evenly among the 4 squares of a sandwich maker.
3. Cook for 3 minutes.
4. Fold in half and add cheese in the middle.

198. Honey Cinnamon Oatmeal

Prep Time: 5 Minutes
Cooking Time: 25 Minutes
Ingredients
- 4 sachet Indonesian Cinnamon and Honey Hot Cereal
- 1/2 tsp Baking Powder
- 3 tbsp Liquid Egg Substitute
- 1 cup Unsweetened Almond Milk
- 11/3 oz Pecans (optional)*
- 11/3 oz Walnuts (optional)*
- 1/4 tsp Cinnamon
- 4 (4.2) oz mini mason jars
- 1 can Cooking spray

Directions:
1. Preheat oven to 350*F.
2. In a large bowl, combine Indonesian Cinnamon and Honey Hot Cereal and baking powder.
3. Add liquid egg white and almond milk; stir until milk is fully absorbed. Fold in nuts.
4. Divide mixture evenly between 4 lightly-greased mason jars, leaving about 1/2 inch at the top. Sprinkle tops with cinnamon.
5. Bake for 20 to 25 minutes on a small baking sheet, until slightly firm and golden on top.
6. Allow to cool completely.
7. Place on lid, refrigerate, ans use within 5 days.

199. Peanut Butter Cups

Prep Time: 15 Minutes
Ingredients
- 2 sachet Essential Decadent Double Chocolate Brownie
- 10 tbsp Unsweetened Vanilla Almond Milk divided
- 10 tbsp Cashew Milk divided
- 1/4 cup Powdered Peanut Butter

Instructions
1. In a small bowl, combine Decadent Double Chocolate Brownie with 6 tablespoons almond milk (or cashew milk) until smooth; set aside.
2. In a separate small bowl, combine powdered peanut butter an remaining almond milk (or cashew milk) until smooth and creamy but not too thin.
3. Place brownie and peanut butter mixtures into separate medium to large-sized resealable plastic bags.
4. Cut off a small portion from one tip of each bag to create piping bags.
5. Pipe brownie mixture to fill bottom third of 20 slots of a mini circular or heart shaped silicone baking mold.
6. Pipe a small amount of peanut butter on top of the brownie in the center of each slot.
7. Pipe remaining brownie mixture on top of the peanut butter to cover the peanut butter and fill each slot.
8. Freeze until firm, at least 2 hours.

200. Tomato Bread

Prep Time: 15 Minutes
Cooking Time: 10 Minutes
Ingredients:
- 1 Cream of Tomato Soup
- 1/4 tsp Baking Powder
- 2 tbsp Water

Options:
- 1/4 cup shredded reduced fat cheese
- 1 Light Laughing Cow Cheese Wedge

Directions:
1. Preheat oven to 425 degrees.
2. Spray a cookie sheet with pam or use parchment paper.
3. Combine soup, baking powder, seasonings and water. Spread the batter on prepared cookie sheet and form a circle.
4. I wet my hands and used them to spread the batter because the batter kept sticking to my spoon. Bake for 5 minutes and then flip using a spatula.
5. If you would like to add cheese, do it now after flipping.
6. Stick the bread back in the oven for 5 more minutes.
7. If using laughing cow cheese, spread it on when the bread is done baking.

LEAN AND GREEN MEAL PLAN 5&1

The Lean and Green 5-and-1 plan requires dieters to eat six small meals a day.
This healthy eating habit promotes weight loss and ensures that dieters have sufficient energy throughout the day.
Five out of the six meals consist of Lean and
Green "Fuelings". The sixth meal of the day is a homemade meal using the "Lean and Green" meal guidelines. For weight loss, most people start with the Optimal Weight 5&1 Plan, which is an 800–1,000 calorie regimen said to help you drop 12 pounds (5.4 kg) over 12 weeks.
This plan also includes 1 optional snack per day, which must be approved by your coach. Plan-approved snacks include 3 celery sticks, 1/2 cup (60 grams) of sugar-free gelatin, or 1/2 ounce (14 grams) of nuts

LEAN AND GREEN MEAL PLAN 4&2&1

A 4-and-2-and-1 plan is an excellent option for those who prefer a less stringent diet and more flexible meal plans to reach their weight loss goals. The Plan is most suitable for those who:
 Want to continue incorporating all of the food groups (including fruits, dairy, and starches) in their meals
- Have type 1 diabetes and are closely supervised by a healthcare provider
- Have type 2 diabetes
- They are sixty-five years or older and rarely engage in exercise or similar activities
- Have less than fifteen pounds (6.8 kilograms) of weight to lose.

This meal plan works similarly to the 5-and-1 meal plan; however, the ratios are different. In this Plan, dieters would eat four "Fuelings", two "Lean and Green" homemade meals, and one healthy snack. Dieters would still be required to eat six times per day or every two to three hours. Some of the Lean and Green approved snacks that I love to munch on include puffed sweet and salty snacks, puffed ranch snacks, olive oil and sea salt popcorn, and sharp cheddar and sour cream popcorn. Sometimes, I prefer making my homemade snacks instead, allowing me to practice my culinary skills. On the 4-and-2-and-1 plan, I can consume one starch, fruit, or dairy snack a day. Below are a few examples of servings for each type of snack:

(5 & 1) Week 1

MONDAY	<ul><li>Spring Green Smoothie Breakfast Drink</li><li>Nectarine And Avocado Smoothie</li><li>Morning Green Juice</li><li>Peanut Butter Green Smoothie</li><li>Pistachio Muffins</li><li>**Asian-Style Tuna Salad Recipe (Lean & Green)**</li></ul>
TUESDAY	<ul><li>Skillet Mexican Zucchini</li><li>Coconut Green Smoothie</li><li>Tiramisu Shake</li><li>Cumin and Cheese Hack</li><li>Cauliflower Wings</li><li>**Vegan Zuppa Toscana (Lean & Green)**</li></ul>
WEDNESDAY	<ul><li>Zucchini Bread</li><li>Oatmeal Cookies</li><li>Mint Cookies</li><li>Shrimp Salad</li><li>Peanut Butter Cookies</li><li>**Heavenly Green Beans And Garlic (Lean & Green)**</li></ul>
THURSDAY	<ul><li>Peanut Brownie and Greek Yogurt</li><li>Cheese Tomato Sandwich</li><li>Honey Cinnamon Oatmeal</li><li>Peanut Butter Cups</li><li>Tomato Bread</li><li>**Roasted Chicken With Lemon Dill Radishes (Lean & Green)**</li></ul>
FRIDAY	<ul><li>Pancake Cinnamon Buns</li><li>Cinnamon Roll</li><li>Pumpkin Pie Custard</li><li>Chocolate Cookies</li><li>Brownie Ice Cream</li><li>**Mexican Chicken Soup (Lean & Green)**</li></ul>
SATURDAY	<ul><li>Oatmeal Cookies</li><li>Mint Cookies</li><li>Shrimp Salad</li><li>Peanut Butter Cookies</li><li>Zucchini Bread</li><li>**Clean And Green Chicken Salad (Lean & Green)**</li></ul>
SUNDAY	<ul><li>Peanut Butter Cookies</li><li>Pumpkin Pie Frappe</li><li>Peanut Butter Brownie</li><li>Pancake Cinnamon Buns</li><li>Cinnamon Roll</li><li>**Keto Green Bean And Chicken Stir Fry (Lean & Green)**</li></ul>

(5 & 1) Week 2

MONDAY	<ul><li>Pecan Ice Cream</li><li>Chocolate Peanut Cup</li><li>Peanut Brownie and Greek Yogurt</li><li>Cheese Tomato Sandwich</li><li>Honey Cinnamon Oatmeal</li><li>**Vegan Zucchini Quinoa Sushi Roll (Lean & Green)**</li></ul>
TUESDAY	<ul><li>Pumpkin Pie Custard</li><li>Chocolate Cookies</li><li>Brownie Ice Cream</li><li>Chocolate Coffee Muffins</li><li>Pancake Muffins</li><li>**Green Goddess Vegan Broccoli Soup (Lean & Green)**</li></ul>
WEDNESDAY	<ul><li>Skillet Mexican Zucchini</li><li>Coconut Green Smoothie</li><li>Tiramisu Shake</li><li>Cumin and Cheese Hack</li><li>Cauliflower Wings</li><li>**Pesto Zucchini Noodles Shrimps & Feta (Lean & Green)**</li></ul>
THURSDAY	<ul><li>Peanut Brownie and Greek Yogurt</li><li>Cheese Tomato Sandwich</li><li>Honey Cinnamon Oatmeal</li><li>Peanut Butter Cups</li><li>Tomato Bread</li><li>**Spinach Pesto With Couscous And Shrimp (Lean & Green)**</li></ul>
FRIDAY	<ul><li>Shrimp Salad</li><li>Peanut Butter Cookies</li><li>Pumpkin Pie Frappe</li><li>Peanut Butter Brownie</li><li>Pancake Cinnamon Buns</li><li>**Thai Cashew Chicken (Lean & Green)**</li></ul>
SATURDAY	<ul><li>Nectarine And Avocado Smoothie</li><li>Morning Green Juice</li><li>Peanut Butter Green Smoothie</li><li>Pistachio Muffins</li><li>Coconut Green Smoothie</li><li>**Chicken Fajitas (Lean & Green)**</li></ul>
SUNDAY	<ul><li>Nectarine And Avocado Smoothie</li><li>Morning Green Juice</li><li>Peanut Butter Green Smoothie</li><li>Pistachio Muffins</li><li>Skillet Mexican Zucchini</li><li>**Lean Green Chicken Pesto Pasta (Lean & Green)**</li></ul>

(5 & 1) Week 3

MONDAY	<ul><li>Tiramisu Shake</li><li>Cumin and Cheese Hack</li><li>Cauliflower Wings</li><li>Neapolitan Popsicles</li><li>Mint Chocolate Muffins</li><li>All Green Chicken Fritters (Lean & Green)</li></ul>
TUESDAY	<ul><li>Pumpkin Pie Frappe</li><li>Peanut Butter Brownie</li><li>Pancake Cinnamon Buns</li><li>Cinnamon Roll</li><li>Pumpkin Pie Custard</li><li>Chopped Green Chicken Salad Recipe (Lean & Green)</li></ul>
WEDNESDAY	<ul><li>Peanut Butter Cookies</li><li>Pumpkin Pie Frappe</li><li>Peanut Butter Brownie</li><li>Pancake Cinnamon Buns</li><li>Cinnamon Roll</li><li>Garlic Chicken With Zoodles (Lean & Green)</li></ul>
THURSDAY	<ul><li>Pistachio Muffins</li><li>Skillet Mexican Zucchini</li><li>Coconut Green Smoothie</li><li>Tiramisu Shake</li><li>Cumin and Cheese Hack</li><li>Spinach Salad With Chicken And Farro (Lean & Green)</li></ul>
FRIDAY	<ul><li>Chocolate Coffee Muffins</li><li>Pancake Muffins</li><li>Pecan Ice Cream</li><li>Chocolate Peanut Cup</li><li>Peanut Brownie and Greek Yogurt</li><li>Clean And Green Chicken Salad (Lean & Green)</li></ul>
SATURDAY	<ul><li>Pumpkin Pie Frappe</li><li>Peanut Butter Brownie</li><li>Pancake Cinnamon Buns</li><li>Cinnamon Roll</li><li>Forager's Nettle Pesto (Lean & Green)</li></ul>
SUNDAY	<ul><li>Pistachio Muffins</li><li>Skillet Mexican Zucchini</li><li>Coconut Green Smoothie</li><li>Tiramisu Shake</li><li>Cumin and Cheese Hack</li><li>The Best Vegan Pesto Recipe (Lean & Green)</li></ul>

(5 & 1) Week 4

MONDAY	<ul><li>Spring Green Smoothie Breakfast Drink</li><li>Nectarine And Avocado Smoothie</li><li>Morning Green Juice</li><li>Peanut Butter Green Smoothie</li><li>Pistachio Muffins</li><li>Asian-Style Tuna Salad Recipe (Lean & Green)</li></ul>
TUESDAY	<ul><li>Chocolate Coffee Muffins</li><li>Pancake Muffins</li><li>Pecan Ice Cream</li><li>Chocolate Peanut Cup</li><li>Peanut Brownie and Greek Yogurt</li><li>Toasted Sesame Ginger Chicken (Lean & Green)</li></ul>
WEDNESDAY	<ul><li>Cinnamon Roll</li><li>Pumpkin Pie Custard</li><li>Chocolate Cookies</li><li>Brownie Ice Cream</li><li>Chocolate Coffee Muffins</li><li>Lean Green Burger (Lean & Green)</li></ul>
THURSDAY	<ul><li>Pecan Ice Cream</li><li>Chocolate Peanut Cup</li><li>Peanut Brownie and Greek Yogurt</li><li>Cheese Tomato Sandwich</li><li>Honey Cinnamon Oatmeal</li><li>Pesto Zucchini Noodles Shrimps & Feta (Lean & Green)</li></ul>
FRIDAY	<ul><li>Peanut Butter Cookies</li><li>Pumpkin Pie Frappe</li><li>Peanut Butter Brownie</li><li>Pancake Cinnamon Buns</li><li>Cinnamon Roll</li><li>Lean Green Bean Salad (Lean & Green)</li></ul>
SATURDAY	<ul><li>Peanut Brownie and Greek Yogurt</li><li>Cheese Tomato Sandwich</li><li>Honey Cinnamon Oatmeal</li><li>Peanut Butter Cups</li><li>Thai Sweet Chili Salmon Soba Noodles (Lean & Green)</li></ul>
SUNDAY	<ul><li>Cinnamon Roll</li><li>Pumpkin Pie Custard</li><li>Chocolate Cookies</li><li>Brownie Ice Cream</li><li>Chocolate Coffee Muffins</li><li>Simple Taco Salad (Lean & Green)</li></ul>

(4&2&1) Week 1

MONDAY	<ul><li>Spring Green Smoothie Breakfast Drink</li><li>Nectarine And Avocado Smoothie</li><li>Morning Green Juice</li><li>Peanut Butter Green Smoothie</li><li>Crepes With Pan-Roasted Vegetables (Lean & Green)</li><li>Asian-Style Tuna Salad Recipe (Lean & Green)</li><li>Holy Guacamole Recipe (Snack)</li></ul>
TUESDAY	<ul><li>Skillet Mexican Zucchini</li><li>Coconut Green Smoothie</li><li>Tiramisu Shake</li><li>Cumin and Cheese Hack</li><li>Spinach Crepes With Pan-Roasted Vegetables (Lean & Green)</li><li>Vegan Zuppa Toscana (Lean & Green)</li><li>Okonomiyaki (Snack)</li></ul>
WEDNESDAY	<ul><li>Zucchini Bread</li><li>Oatmeal Cookies</li><li>Mint Cookies</li><li>Shrimp Salad</li><li>Crispy Kohlrabi Slaw (Lean & Green)</li><li>Heavenly Green Beans And Garlic (Lean & Green)</li><li>Spinach Crepes With Pan-Roasted Vegetables (Snack)</li></ul>
THURSDAY	<ul><li>Peanut Brownie and Greek Yogurt</li><li>Cheese Tomato Sandwich</li><li>Honey Cinnamon Oatmeal</li><li>Peanut Butter Cups</li><li>Medifast Lean And Green Recipe (Lean & Green)</li><li>Roasted Chicken With Lemon Dill Radishes (Lean & Green)</li><li>Crispy Kohlrabi Slaw (Snack)</li></ul>
FRIDAY	<ul><li>Pancake Cinnamon Buns</li><li>Cinnamon Roll</li><li>Pumpkin Pie Custard</li><li>Chocolate Cookies</li><li>Green Goddess Vegan Broccoli Soup (Lean & Green)</li><li>Mexican Chicken Soup (Lean & Green)</li><li>Muffins florentine recipe (Snack)</li></ul>
SATURDAY	<ul><li>Oatmeal Cookies</li><li>Mint Cookies</li><li>Shrimp Salad</li><li>Peanut Butter Cookies</li><li>Vegan Broccoli Pesto Pasta (Lean & Green)</li><li>Clean And Green Chicken Salad (Lean & Green)</li><li>Avocado Goat Cheese Cucumber Appetizers (Snack)</li></ul>
SUNDAY	<ul><li>Peanut Butter Cookies</li><li>Pumpkin Pie Frappe</li><li>Peanut Butter Brownie</li><li>Pancake Cinnamon Buns</li><li>Winter Coleslaw With Barberries (Lean & Green)</li><li>Keto Green Bean And Chicken Stir Fry (Lean & Green)</li><li>Zucchini Tart With Ricotta And Herbs (Snack)</li></ul>

(4&2&1) Week 2

MONDAY	• Spring Green Smoothie Breakfast Drink • Nectarine And Avocado Smoothie • Morning Green Juice • Peanut Butter Green Smoothie • Healthy Baked Zucchini Fritter (Lean & Green) • Asian-Style Tuna Salad Recipe (Lean & Green) • Tex-Mex Seared Salmon (Snack)
TUESDAY	• Skillet Mexican Zucchini • Coconut Green Smoothie • Tiramisu Shake • Cumin and Cheese Hack • Cashew Chicken & Cauliflower Rice (Lean & Green) • Vegan Zuppa Toscana (Lean & Green) • Fresh Pico De Gallo (Snack)
WEDNESDAY	• Zucchini Bread • Oatmeal Cookies • Mint Cookies • Shrimp Salad • Keto green bean and chicken stir fry (Lean & Green) • Heavenly Green Beans And Garlic (Lean & Green) • Fresh Lime Crema (Snack)
THURSDAY	• Peanut Brownie and Greek Yogurt • Cheese Tomato Sandwich • Honey Cinnamon Oatmeal • Peanut Butter Cups • Chicken Fajita Lettuce Wraps (Lean & Green) • Roasted Chicken With Lemon Dill Radishes (Lean & Green) • Low Carb Sloppy Joes (Snack)
FRIDAY	• Pancake Cinnamon Buns • Cinnamon Roll • Pumpkin Pie Custard • Chocolate Cookies • Greek Lemon Chicken Soup • Mexican Chicken Soup (Lean & Green) • Lemon Dill Roasted Radishes (Snack)
SATURDAY	• Oatmeal Cookies • Mint Cookies • Shrimp Salad • Peanut Butter Cookies • Lean Green Chicken Soup (Lean & Green) • Clean And Green Chicken Salad (Lean & Green) • Okonomiyaki (Snack)
SUNDAY	• Peanut Butter Cookies • Pumpkin Pie Frappe • Peanut Butter Brownie • Pancake Cinnamon Buns • Cinnamon Roll (Lean & Green) • Keto Green Bean And Chicken Stir Fry (Lean & Green) • Zucchini Tart With Ricotta And Herbs (Snack)

(4&2&1) Week 3

MONDAY	- Spring Green Smoothie Breakfast Drink - Nectarine And Avocado Smoothie - Morning Green Juice - Peanut Butter Green Smoothie - Chicken Pad Thai Recipe (Lean & Green) - Asian-Style Tuna Salad Recipe (Lean & Green) - Fresh Pico De Gallo
TUESDAY	- Skillet Mexican Zucchini - Coconut Green Smoothie - Tiramisu Shake - Cumin and Cheese Hack - Green Chiles Chicken Squash Boats (Lean & Green) - Vegan Zuppa Toscana (Lean & Green) - Lemon Dill Roasted Radishes
WEDNESDAY	- Zucchini Bread - Oatmeal Cookies - Mint Cookies - Shrimp Salad - Low-Carb Green Smoothie (Lean & Green) - Heavenly Green Beans And Garlic (Lean & Green) - Zucchini Tart With Ricotta And Herbs
THURSDAY	- Peanut Brownie and Greek Yogurt - Cheese Tomato Sandwich - Honey Cinnamon Oatmeal - Peanut Butter Cups - Healthy Cream Of Broccoli Soup (Lean & Green) - Roasted Chicken With Lemon Dill Radishes (Lean & Green) - Muffins florentine recipe
FRIDAY	- Pancake Cinnamon Buns - Cinnamon Roll - Pumpkin Pie Custard - Chocolate Cookies - Spring Vegetable Zoodle Pasta (Lean & Green) - Mexican Chicken Soup (Lean & Green) - Crispy Kohlrabi Slaw
SATURDAY	- Oatmeal Cookies - Mint Cookies - Shrimp Salad - Peanut Butter Cookies - Lean Green Burger (Lean & Green) - Clean And Green Chicken Salad (Lean & Green) - Oatmeal Cookies
SUNDAY	- Peanut Butter Cookies - Pumpkin Pie Frappe - Peanut Butter Brownie - Pancake Cinnamon Buns - Summer Zoodle Primavera (Lean & Green) - Keto Green Bean And Chicken Stir Fry (Lean & Green) - Zucchini Tart With Ricotta And Herbs

(4&2&1) Week 4

MONDAY	• Spring Green Smoothie Breakfast Drink • Nectarine And Avocado Smoothie • Morning Green Juice • Peanut Butter Green Smoothie • Green Chicken Enchilada Casserole (Lean & Green) • Asian-Style Tuna Salad Recipe (Lean & Green) • Muffins florentine recipe
TUESDAY	• Skillet Mexican Zucchini • Coconut Green Smoothie • Tiramisu Shake • Cumin and Cheese Hack • Clean And Green Chicken Salad (Lean & Green) • Vegan Zuppa Toscana (Lean & Green) • Muffins florentine recipe
WEDNESDAY	• Zucchini Bread • Oatmeal Cookies • Mint Cookies • Shrimp Salad • Minute Meal-Prep Chicken, Rice And Broccoli (Lean & Green) • Heavenly Green Beans And Garlic (Lean & Green) • Lemon Dill Roasted Radishes
THURSDAY	• Peanut Brownie and Greek Yogurt • Cheese Tomato Sandwich • Honey Cinnamon Oatmeal • Peanut Butter Cups • Tomato Bread (Lean & Green) • Roasted Chicken With Lemon Dill Radishes (Lean & Green) • Fresh Pico De Gallo
FRIDAY	• Pancake Cinnamon Buns • Cinnamon Roll • Pumpkin Pie Custard • Chocolate Cookies • One Skillet Italian Chicken (Lean & Green) • Mexican Chicken Soup (Lean & Green) • Crispy Kohlrabi Slaw
SATURDAY	• Oatmeal Cookies • Mint Cookies • Shrimp Salad • Peanut Butter Cookies • Healthy Mongolian Chicken (Lean & Green) • Clean And Green Chicken Salad (Lean & Green) • Tex-Mex Seared Salmon
SUNDAY	• Peanut Butter Cookies • Pumpkin Pie Frappe • Peanut Butter Brownie • Pancake Cinnamon Buns • Mexican Chicken Soup (Lean & Green) • Keto Green Bean And Chicken Stir Fry (Lean & Green) • Fresh Pico De Gallo